PRAISE FROM UNCOMMON WOMEN FOR

Bachelor Girls

by WENDY WASSERSTEIN

"Wendy Wasserstein—the *only* logical one to succeed Dorothy Parker, Lillian Hellman, and Eleanor
Roosevelt."

—Swoosie Kurtz

"I can think of no other writer who makes me laugh and
cry with such frequency as Wendy Wasserstein does.
Her writing reveals the perils and pleasures of being
alive with a unique combination of honesty, wit, and
compassion. She's glorious."

—Joan Allen

"Reading Wendy Wasserstein is not just fun, it's
therapeutic—like having lunch with your best girlfriends and laughing yourself silly. Whether you're a
bachelor girl or not, you'll recognize yourself somewhere in this book."

—Jill Eikenberry

Bachelor Girls

WENDY WASSERSTEIN

Bachelor Girls

VINTAGE BOOKS
A DIVISION OF RANDOM HOUSE, INC.
NEW YORK

FIRST VINTAGE BOOKS EDITION, JUNE 1991

Copyright © 1984, 1985, 1986, 1987, 1988, 1989, 1990 by Wendy Wasserstein

Most of the pieces in this book were originally published, in slightly
different form, in one of the following publications: *Elle*, *Gentlemen's
Quarterly*, *New York Woman*, and *The New York Times*.
"Tokyo Story" was originally published as "Opening Night Nippon Style" in
Travel & Leisure, American Express Publishing, April 1988.
Grateful acknowledgment is made to the following for permission to
reprint previously published material:
Art & Antiques: "She Ate Cake with Marie Antoinette," originally published as
"Portraits by a Lady," in *Art & Antiques*, September 1989.
Reprinted with permission.
Frank Music Corp.: Excerpt from "Take Back Your Mink" from *Guys and Dolls*
by Frank Loesser. Copyright 1950 by Frank Music Corp. Copyright
renewed 1978 by Frank Music Corp. International copyright secured.
All rights reserved. Used by permission.
Warner/Chappell Music, Inc.: Excerpt from "My Fair Lady" by Alan Jay Lerner
and Frederick Loewe. Copyright © 1956 by Alan Jay Lerner, Frederick Loewe,
and Chappell & Co., Inc. All rights reserved. Used by permission.

Library of Congress Cataloging-in-Publication Data
Wasserstein, Wendy.
Bachelor girls / Wendy Wasserstein.—1st Vintage Books ed.
p.   cm.
Reprint. Originally published: New York: Knopf, 1990.
ISBN 0-679-73062-1
1. Single women—Humor.   I. Title.
[PS3573.A798B34   1991]
814'.54—dc20   90-55682
CIP

Designed by Iris Weinstein

Manufactured in the United States of America
10   9   8   7   6   5

To Harriet, Mary Jane, and, always, Susan
girlfriends

bach·e·lor (bach′ ə ler, bach′lər), *n.* **3.** a fur seal, esp. a young male, kept from the breeding grounds by the older males.

bach′elor girl′, an unmarried woman, esp. a young one, who supports herself and often lives alone. [1890–95]

—*The Random House Dictionary of the English Language,* Second Edition, Unabridged

Acknowledgments

I have never understood the phrase "without whose help this book would not have been possible." All I know is that this book is possible because of Betsy Carter and *New York Woman* magazine; Terry Adams; Arlene Donovan; Mike Leahy; Pamela Fiori; Mitch Kohn and Karl Lott, whose ability to read my handwriting is miraculous; and Kay Feibleman and Tom Flaherty, who provided me with a room of my own on New Light Lane.

Thanks also to André Bishop, Lynda Lee Burks, Anne Cattaneo, Christopher Durang, William Finn, Martha Friedman, Aimee Garn, Cathy and Stephen Graham, Gerald Gutierrez, Michiko Kakutani, Heidi Landesman, James Lapine, William Ivey Long, Terrence McNally, Peter Parnell, Pat Quinn, Carole Rothman, Paul Rudnick, Daniel Sullivan, and my family, without whose help this book would not have been possible.

Contents

Bachelor Girl   3

The World's Worst Boyfriends   9

My Mother, Then and NOW   15

The Body Minimal   23

Tokyo Story   29

Nails: The Naked and the Red   39

Aunt Florence's Bar Mitzvah   45

The Sleeping Beauty Syndrome:
The New Agony of Single Men   53

Modern Maturity   61

Reflections on Leather Rhinos   67

Perfect Women Who Are Bearable   75

Big Brother   81

She Ate Cake with Marie Antoinette   85

CONTENTS

A Screenwriter's Diary   91

The Good, the Plaid, and the Ugly   101

To Live and Diet   107

High Adventure in the Balkans   113

The New Capitalist Tool   125

Pappagallo Jungle   131

The Razor's Edge   137

The Messiah   143

A Phone of Her Own   149

Avenue of the Stars   155

In Charm's Way   165

Mrs. Smith Goes to Washington   175

Jean Harlow's Wedding Night   181

Christmas in Flatbush   189

Winner Take All   193

Boy Meets Girl   199

Bachelor Girls

Bachelor Girl

"For it is the Sahara, the vastest, hottest, cruelest
desert on earth. But we must cross it just the same
—1,600 miles, the distance from New York to
Mexico—to reach the next world-wonder I want
you to see."   —Richard Halliburton's
                    Complete Book of Marvels

"There are no ugly women, only lazy ones."
                    —Helena Rubinstein

"So, take back your mink
To from whence it came
And tell them to Hollanderize it
For some other dame."
—Miss Adelaide in Frank Loesser's *Guys and Dolls*

I recall in my early years three major ostensibly unconnected influences: Richard Halliburton's *Complete Book of Marvels*, the Helena Rubinstein Charm School, and Broadway musicals.

Mr. Halliburton's book was a young adventurer's

travel guide to spectacular places around the world, rang-
ing from "New York, City Extraordinary" and "Blue
Grotto, Cavern of Loveliness" to the Taj Mahal and Tim-
buktu. It was a "*magic carpet* to all the wonders of both
the Orient and the Occident." My brother was given the
book as a Bar Mitzvah gift, and I stole it from him.

On my own thirteenth birthday, I did not receive a
junior Baedecker guide to the Tigris and Euphrates. Believing that the coming-of-age needs of girls and boys dif-
fer, my mother signed me up for one-on-one personal
training at the Helena Rubinstein Charm School. Under
the tutelage of that great lady's disciples I learned the
importance of pampering my feet and of never carrying a
schoolbag on my shoulders, as well as how to get in and
out of a taxi by sliding the derrière in first. The sole
charm-school skill I've retained is the taxi maneuver,
whose execution, frankly, depends a great deal on the
driver.

As a child the ultimate transport for me, even beyond
the *Complete Book of Marvels,* was attending a matinee
performance of a Broadway musical. Nothing could compare to that exhilarating moment of joy and anticipation
when the lights go down and the orchestra strikes up.

I mention these touchstones because their influence
seems to be reflected in the eclectic nature of this book.
The topics considered in the following pages range from
the return of the manicure (the realm of the beauteous
Madame Rubinstein) to an international children's chess
tournament in Timişoara, Rumania (Halliburtonian high
adventure in the Balkans), and a production of *Les Misérables* in Tokyo.

I have, in fact, combed these pieces in search of their
commonality. Or, as Abe Burrows, the librettist of *Guys
and Dolls,* once put it more bluntly, "You gotta have a

tree to hang the bananas on." Most of the bananas herein were written over the past five years on assignment for magazines, many of them for a monthly column entitled "The Meaning of Life" in *New York Woman*. So what the pieces have in common more than anything else—their tree, as it were—is a point of view.

I hasten to acknowledge that there are more urgent world issues to be discussed than shopping with men, telephones, and my mother. But about these particular matters I seem to have an opinion. And both the joy and the curse of magazine writing is having a deadline to express these opinions at what seems their moment of clarity. In other words, there's no reason or excuse to postpone gratification.

As with any book that contains observations on the world's worst boyfriends, the curator of the Metropolitan Museum of Art, and body hair, the circumstances are probably best explained by Schopenhauer. According to the great philosopher, "Every man takes the limits of his own field of vision for the limits of the world." In the case of this book, the particular field of vision is not one man's but one woman's, and the woman just happens to be a Bachelor Girl. Wouldn't Schopenhauer be surprised!

The term Bachelor Girl is perhaps easier to explain. Whenever I managed to escape third grade due to tonsilitis or by placing scalding water on my tongue while my mother was preparing the thermometer, I would spend the day watching television. My favorite morning program—and there were such classics as "Our Miss Brooks," "My Little Margie," and "I Married Joan'" in that illustrious lineup—was "Bachelor Father." As I recall, the situation of this comedy involved John Forsythe (thirty years before his "Dynasty" marriage to both Joan Collins and Linda Evans) living alone with his pony-tailed daughter and an Asian houseboy. I don't know whether it was having a father who frequently wore white dinner jackets or the prospect of never having to show a report card to a demanding mother that most appealed to me, but the triumvirate of dashing daddy, hassled houseboy, and darling pony-tailed daughter seemed to me the ultimate in urbanity and sophistication. None of my friends in third grade at The Yeshiva Flatbush came home to an Asian houseboy.

Bachelor Father was debonair, suave, a small-screen, prime-time Cary Grant. And to my eyes this eligible bachelor, well-bred and desirable, seemed a viable role model —despite the gender obstacle. In other words, I knew I'd rather wear a dinner jacket than perform the routine housewifely duties of Mrs. Danny Thomas, Mrs. Father Knows Best, or especially June Cleaver. In third grade, I was already certain that at no time in my life would I ever live in a house as neat or wear stockings as often as the women in those shows did. Danny Thomas got to smoke cigars and be amusing, and Marjorie Lord, the actress who played his wife, got to wear shirtwaists.

So at an early age I developed a keen interest in finding a female counterpart for Bachelor Father: a woman who possessed all the vitality of a Broadway musical, whose charms would beguile even Helena Rubinstein, and who never closed herself off from the possibility of adventure. This is why, as a teenager, I became fascinated by the Doris Day film oeuvre. Whereas my hipper friends in junior high were already hooked on early Dylan and praising the subtlety of Janet Margolin's performance in *David and Lisa,* I privately pondered the social and sexual implications of the cinema of Doris.

In *Lover Come Back,* Doris worked as an advertising executive, she had a bachelorette apartment, she cooked for herself, she spoke up to Rock Hudson, and she even played the role of seductress. In *Pillow Talk,* Doris, an interior decorator, gave up her domestic duties and hired Thelma Ritter as a houseperson. Moreover, she grew so appalled at Hudson's philandering that she vented her rage by decorating his apartment in a highly suggestive leopard-and-leather motif. Far from being a prissy virgin, Ms. Day seemed to me in these films bright, self-motivated, and charming—a female incarnation of my Bachelor Father.

Doris in her heyday was, despite her career-woman status, neither bitter nor desperate nor cold. She was not a spinster who raged against her biological clock or cried herself to sleep because she was still on the shelf at twenty-five. Doris was a gal on the town, a metropolitan *mensch* with a rich, full life. (Of course her life always became richer and fuller at the end of the film when she dropped her bachelorette apartment, and her career, and even Thelma Ritter, in order to move in with the formerly philandering Rock Hudson, now magically overhauled and awakened to his consuming love for Doris.)

Since I've now moved from Schopenhauer to Doris Day, the eclectic nature of this book should be self-evident. I will attempt to connect the dots.

In Doris's "Bachelor Girl" films, she never regretted her choices, she just went about her life with innate high spirits. Of course, Doris's was an earlier, less complicated time than ours. Yet there is still something distinctly appealing, dignified, even glamorous, to me about the life of a Bachelor Girl, from her morning make-up routine to her travels to her moments of sadness. (I know some will flinch at the mere mention of the word "girl."

Frankly, when I worked part-time as a stenographer in an office and people referred to me as "the girl," I did. Furthermore, the reason grown-up women are most often called "girl" is to underscore their incompleteness: They're husbandless. But I believe it would be a mistake to overlook the word's positive connotations. Girlishness suggests not only innocence or coquettishness but also exuberance, flair, and potential.) I don't much like to think that being a Bachelor Girl limits how you see the world. On the other hand, I know that it certainly limits how the world sees you. This book offers a glimpse of the world from one Bachelor Girl's perspective.

In all honesty, it's hard to rid oneself of the belief that someday a prince will come along. But, for me at least, there are many days when I'm delighted to wake up alone in my apartment. What I often do then, as a matter of habit, is put on my white dinner jacket, slide into bed derrière first, drop the record needle on *Guys and Dolls,* dust off my purloined copy of the *Complete Book of Marvels,* and summon the houseboy to bring me a simple, perfectly lovely Bachelor Girl breakfast in bed.

The World's Worst Boyfriends

A friend of mine recently woke up in the middle of the night to find her new boyfriend weeping. "What's wrong, honey? Are you OK? Can I get you something?" My friend saw a big future with this guy and was willing to abandon everything, even sleep, to please him. "Do you want to talk about it, dear?"

He looked at her, his dark brown eyes welling with tears. "I was watching you while you were sleeping."

Yes, she thought, *and you love me so much it was overwhelming.*

"And I couldn't help thinking that you look just like my Aunt Lotte who lives in Kew Gardens and never had a date in her life. It made me sad. Deeply, deeply sad."

Now this friend, who in no way resembles Aunt Lotte,

knows there are better candidates out there. She knows there are available, sensitive, attractive men. According to the latest *People* magazine survey, there are at least three of them. And every healthy girl with a healthy sense of self should pull herself together, raise her hemline, and find them. Just ask any best-selling therapist/nutritionist/author from San Diego.

But before any Bachelor Girl undertakes such a search, she should be allowed one primal scream. I propose that mine take the form of a roundup of the world's worst boyfriends, ever.

Some general rules apply here. First of all, the worst boyfriends are not, on the surface, the meanest boyfriends. Most girls don't meet Bluebeard on a first date and think, *Sure he's a little nasty and a little sly, but he's really furry, fuzzy, and cute.* Mean is simple. It's the more complicated stuff that's hazy.

There are very nice men who will happily spend twenty years taking you out to dinner twice a week, to the seashore on summer weekends, and on annual fall leaf-peeping tours of New England, yet when you timidly bring up "moving forward" they explain that they are just beginning to make real progress in therapy, you need to be patient and give them some more time, they really love you but there are a few things they need to work out still. Think of the head cold sweet Nathan Detroit gave to Adelaide in *Guys and Dolls.* She had a permanent case of "La grippe" from getting off the train to Niagara fourteen times.

What distinguishes the contestants in the W.B.E. (Worst Boyfriends Ever) Olympics is their ability to wreak emotional havoc. Where once there was calm, now there is constant tumult and turmoil. Today is Tuesday

—that means he likes me. Tuesday is our good day. Especially if I haven't seen him since Saturday. I wonder if I'll ever get him on Wednesday. I guess I ought to prepare. I'll cancel the doctor, the ballet, and the drink with that third available man from the survey. I have to keep my nights open. Just in case.

Another distinguishing trait of worst boyfriends is their "Dear Occupant" behavior. In other words, they don't do anything as obvious as raise their voices. They don't stamp their feet or throw toast. They simply decide that you have ceased to exist (poof! no more! all gone!). Fear of intimacy is understandable; being treated like junk mail is insufferable.

Triangles. Ask a worst boyfriend and he'll admit that the triangle is his favorite configuration. There's safety and torture in isosceles. A triangle means there's always another angle who's less threatening (or more threatening), prettier and smarter (or less pretty and less smart). Contrary to popular belief and geometric theory, it's easier to deal with hexagonists. Then you're just *e pluribus unum*—one out of many. Which is to say, he's clearly a philanderer and you're maybe long-suffering but otherwise clearly perfect.

The worse the boyfriend, the more stunning your American Express bill. Since the worst boyfriends have keen and critical eyes, you have to shine for them, dress for them, coif for them, and, in California, liposuct for them. And there's nothing like primping for an uninterested party. Consider the case of the wretched Mathilde in Stendhal's *The Red and the Black*. She had her daddy, the marquis, offer her beloved Julien a fortune and a title just so he'd like her a little bit. No dice—he still preferred Madame de Rênal. But, of course, Mathilde was an extremist. She buried the head of her worst boyfriend.

Obviously, the worst boyfriends, like Julien, can

cause disastrous side effects. Low self-esteem, low energy, low humor, in fact low everything except calorie-intake are standard symptoms of a W.B.E. relationship. And it spirals. "Oh God, will all my boyfriends be worst boyfriends? Do I do something that attracts the worst boyfriends? Do they give one another my number? Do I really look like Aunt Lotte who never had a date in her life?" Finally, there's the ultimate self-recrimination: "If I were really good, I wouldn't have a worst boyfriend."

Forget it! The point is, it's not our fault. It's theirs. They've been this way for centuries. Worst boyfriends are not a new phenomenon. Six healthy gals in a row all thought they could change Henry VIII. (Henry, by the way, is only a semifinalist in the W.B.E. Olympics. He has points deducted for [1] actually marrying the ladies and [2] being happy for a time.)

Historians from Thucydides to Will and Ariel Durant urge us to learn from our mistakes. And moralists from Sophocles to Gary Hart agree. There's knowledge in history. Therefore, in the hope that tomorrow's therapist/nutritionists will all be able to assert that "Smart Women Make Brilliant Choices," I offer this selective sampling of fellas from whom a lesson or two can be learned. (And next time you get fixed up with Prince Hamlet or someone who was meant to be, be polite, say, "Hello. I see that you're very attractive, sensitive, and Danish. But I am personally not interested in madness or drowning. Go be a rogue and a peasant slave with some other dame.")

Here are the gold medalists in the W.B.E. Olympics:

1. Aethelred the Unready. King of England (968?–1016). Don't ask.
2. Gennaro Borgia. The son of Lucrezia Borgia. Not a family man, and just imagine being home for the holidays with him and Mom.

3. James Boswell. What woman wants to follow around a man following around Samuel Johnson?
4. Oliver Cromwell. Picky, picky.
5. The Reverend Arthur Dimmesdale. After years of letting Hester Prynne take the rap, he *finally* made a public confession. Thank you very much, Arthur.
6. Johan August Strindberg. Definite girl problems. Invented "Dear Occupant" behavior prior to the advent of the mail-order catalog.
7. Grigori Yefimovich Rasputin. An affair is one thing, but a mystic who brings down an entire dynasty is something else. It took poisoned tea cakes, lethal wine, bullets, and being submerged in icy waters to destroy him. Worst boyfriends know a meal ticket when they see one.
8. Brigham Young. Said to have had twenty-seven wives. There *is* a point of no return.
9. Dr. Herman Tarnower. Never write your boyfriend's term papers.
10. Mel Gibson. A happily married family man. The impossible dream.

And if ever you find yourself involved with a boyfriend you think couldn't be worse, just remember that some other Bachelor Girl once canceled the doctor, the ballet, and the date to sit home and wait for Claus von Bülow to call.

My Mother, Then and NOW

They gave my mother an award. I have spent fifteen years in therapy talking about this woman and the National Organization for Women gave her an award.

Let me clear this up slightly. My mother did not receive the NOW Legal Defense and Education Fund BUDDY (Bringing Up Daughters Differently) Award for being the first mother in space. She has not juggled her time between her thriving orthodontia practice and raising four children. Nor has she devoted her life to charity and earned a thirty-year remarkable service salute. She did not struggle as a secretary, a gardener, or a seamstress to make my education possible. My mother got an award for being my mother. In order words, the NOW-LDEF gave her an award for raising me.

Actually, my mother got the award for raising not only me but also my sisters, Sandra and Georgette. Our mother's BUDDY award celebrates "the accomplishment and vision of families in which gender was never a stumbling block and equality for sons and daughters was considered a birthright." My sister Sandra is a mother and a businesswoman—a pioneer, in fact, who was at one point president of the card division of American Express. Georgette lives in Vermont, where she is an innkeeper, and has raised four children, the last of whom was born when Georgette was forty. I am a playwright. My mother, therefore, raised a variety pack: a mainstream corporate executive, a New England homemaker, and a solo artist. From the point of view of child diversity, gender was never a stumbling block.

My mother and I go way back.

When I was in second grade my brother and I cut the cherries off our mother's spring bonnet. Then, seized by the "I cannot tell a lie" legend of our founding forefather, I persuaded my brother to confess. Our attempt to justify the deed revealed a lot more about our attitude toward our mother than it did about our presidential prospects.

"We just want you to look like all the other mothers," we said as we presented her with the slashed plastic fruit. "We just want you to be normal."

Lola Wasserstein was never like the other mothers. In an era personified by Donna Reed, my mother preferred Carmen Miranda. As Lola herself so aptly put it, "I like go-go." But unlike Carmen, my mother did not have a creative outlet for her immense energy. Like Donna Reed, she had her family.

Every year my mother would take us to the great

Christmas show at Radio City Music Hall. The queue of grown-ups and children waiting patiently to get in to the show would wrap its way twice around Rockefeller Center. But my mother had no "go-go" to spare. She would walk directly up to the head usher and explain that we were visitors from Kansas and that we were in the city for one day only. (The first time she selected "Kansas" was the day after our family had watched *The Wizard of Oz* on television.) "The one place we really wanted to see was Radio City," she would implore the usher. Looking back, I sometimes can't understand why those ushers didn't tell us to click our heels three times and go home, but they didn't. They always let us in.

Another of Lola's memorable performances was delivered annually in Florida. In the 1950s Arthur Godfrey owned what was rumored to be an anti-Semitic hotel in Miami Beach—a glaring and odious anomaly, almost a contradiction in terms. The Kenilworth was billed as a retreat for those who preferred to be with people from "your own background and taste." Every year my mother would take my brother and me to the front desk at The Kenilworth and ask for directions to "the Cohen Bar Mitzvah." And every year she would be admonished, "Madame, there is no Cohen Bar Mitzvah here." (Years later I lived in the same apartment house as Arthur Godfrey. When, on the day he passed away, an ambulance pulled away from the curb in front of our building, I couldn't help thinking, *He's off to the Cohen Bar Mitzvah in the sky.*)

But the *pièce de résistance* was dinner with Lola at Lüchow's. At what must have been a desperate point in its illustrious history, Lüchow's, the venerable German restaurant on Fourteenth Street, hired an oompah band. This was many years after Diamond Jim Brady had come around for goose, and I guess they needed an angle. Every night, after a rousing chorus of "Ach Du Lieber Augustine" and "Roll Out the Barrel," the oompah band —Tyrolean minstrels wearing lederhosen and carrying accordions—would stroll toward a prescribed table to offer a birthday or anniversary serenade.

It was during this oompah period that my mother decided I was a "shy" child. I was perpetually embarrassed by her Kansas improvisations, and I obviously preferred that she not wear fruited hats. My mother, believing that one must carefully explain a point of view to children, methodically laid out for me Lola's rules of order:

"You can wear diamonds from Tiffany's and look like Klein's basement, or you can wear junk, real *chazerai*" —literally translated: pig food—"from Klein's basement, and if you carry yourself with confidence, head up, chest out, then you'll always look like you're wearing diamonds from Tiffany's."

Clearly, in my shy period I was projecting a very demure Klein's basement, and with the assistance of Lüchow's and the oompah band my mother set out to correct this. Lola was at the forefront of behavior modification.

Our family dined at Lüchow's regularly, and once a month, between bites of sauerkraut and dumplings, my mother would get up from our dinner table and tell the oompah band that it was my birthday. (I still have no idea whether in April the band remembered that I was the girl whose birthday had been celebrated in March.) I would have to sit there, head up, chest out, beaming with pride and confidence as they played "Happy Birthday" on their accordions just for me. Is it any wonder that to this day I have a terminal fear of men wearing lederhosen and tiny feathered caps? Or that I try to enter all social situations wearing neither *chazerai* from Klein's basement nor diamonds from Tiffany's? Even just hearing a few bars of "Happy Birthday" in a restaurant can still cause me to involuntarily excuse myself from the table.

Lola Wasserstein has always made great copy. And she has always lived up to her reputation. At graduate school, I solidified my friendship with my classmate and fellow playwright Christopher Durang by telling him countless "Lola" stories. Of course, I embellished them a little— after all, we were in drama school. But eventually Christopher got the chance to see and experience Lola for himself. She arrived one day at my apartment, unannounced and dressed as Patty Hearst, complete with a beret and toy gun. Lola never disappoints. I wonder how many other of the mothers recognized at the NOW BUDDY lunch have dressed up as members of the Symbionese Liberation Army.

I can't help feeling that my mother is probably one of the most interesting people I'll ever get to know. This is the case partly, I'm sure, because I've spent more time with her and love her more than just about anyone else I'll ever know. But that's not the only reason. My mother's eyes have seen life, yet have never become bitter.

I remember one Passover when my father sat on my mother's lap and, as she kissed him, she said, "We did it! Nine grandchildren!" I wondered at that moment what I would ever accomplish that would make me feel as fulfilled as my mother with her nine grandchildren. I wondered if I'd ever be able to love as totally and selflessly as she does.

But I am leaving out the reign of terror. My mother,

very much like me, is what husbands tend to refer to, kindly, as "high-strung." A tiny incident, a small blow-up, and my mother is circling La Guardia Airport. When I had my first jobs Off-Broadway and I was still living with my parents, I would sometimes come home at 1 a.m. to find my mother awake in bed. I can still see her, the autobiography of Golda Meir in her lap, and her brilliant eyes darting out at me to let me know she couldn't sleep, she couldn't breathe, and, even if I was twenty-four, I was a spoiled and very selfish child.

Although my mother was a renegade in the domestic details of her own life, her position on marriage and family has never wavered. It is intractable. To this day I receive phone calls whose opening lines a writer could spend months inventing. Two of these have become legendary among Lolaologists: (1) "Your sister-in-law is pregnant and that means more to me than a million dollars or any play" and (2) "Now that there's a writers' strike, maybe you should think about Cardozo Law School." The latter may seem mild, but it happened to arrive on the same day that I learned I had won a $10,000 playwriting grant.

I have never doubted my mother's generosity of spirit. I have never doubted that, to the best of her ability, with all her heart and soul, she loves my sisters and me. But it is sometimes difficult for her to understand us on our own terms. What's even more difficult, perhaps impossible, for her is separating herself from us.

On the weekend of my graduation from drama school, I found myself standing with my mother in the dressing room of Ann Taylor's in New Haven. I, who have always favored elastic-waistbanded, non-confining or non-itchy floral skirts and dresses—they are attractive yet not too Dressed for Success, and, most importantly, they cover the territory—was about to try on a garment somewhere between a nightgown and an acceptably free-flowing lily-of-the-valley-print frock. My mother, on the other hand, had her eye on a pink linen suit—an ensemble that, with a few carefully chosen accessories, could look like diamonds from Tiffany's.

So I tried on this pink linen suit. And, once on me, it transmuted very quickly to *chazerai* from Klein's basement. But my mother, steadfast to her goal, opened the dressing room door and asked the saleslady for a larger size. Any spoiled, selfish child can tell you that her worst spoiled, selfish behavior emerges when there's a witness, a third party, to view the display. So as my mother continued to address the saleslady, I grabbed my mother's hand and placed it on my arm.

"Mother, this is me." I then moved her hand to where it had been. "And this is you." I proceeded to move her hand back and forth, back and forth. "There is a separation between us. We are not the same. If you want a pink linen suit, buy yourself a goddamned pink linen suit."

My mother's sparkling eyes darted over me. "I don't know what you want from me!"

I'm not sure whether my mother was crying as she bolted from that dressing room. I know only that I felt the same as when I chopped down that cherry hat. I just wanted her to be like all the other mothers. I had no idea, really, what they were like, but I wanted her to be like them.

I took the letter announcing Lola's BUDDY Award to my current therapist. I mean, I had spent a fortune analyzing the oompah episode and now this arrived—and from the National Organization for Women. They were supposed to be my liberators! Why wasn't this award going to mothers who actually waited on line at Radio City! Why weren't *they* being invited to a luncheon at the Plaza?

There were four other BUDDY families at the Plaza luncheon. The daughters among them included doctors, art curators, filmmakers, mothers, housewives. These were families whose clan gatherings you could imagine without much difficulty: a birthday celebration, say, at a seaside restaurant on Cape Cod—not an oompah band in sight. Theirs were the sort of families I might once have noticed across a restaurant dining room, only to find myself wishing that we were more like them.

Our whole family showed up for my mother's award: my sisters, me, my dad, my brother, and my nieces, Pamela, Samantha, Jennifer, Melissa, and Tajlei. My nieces are lovely young women—two blond, two brunette, and a chess-playing redhead—and all of them spirited, intelligent, and morally grounded. In the next generation gender is not going to be a stumbling block.

As I gazed up and down our table, it struck me that our family actually didn't appear that different from the other BUDDY families. And, in fact, when my mother, looking like diamonds from Tiffany's, walked toward the podium to accept her award, a part of me wished that she had come dressed as Patty Hearst, or that she would announce to everyone in the room that she was from Kansas and visiting the city for one day only.

In a way, I wish the women at that luncheon could know the real reason why they made the right decision when they chose my mother.

The Body
Minimal

This is written for Raquel, Morgan, Jane, Joan, Linda, and Victoria. I want to thank them for helping me enter thirty, approach forty, and commit to a healthier, more vital fifty. Without their guidance, concern, and inspiration, I would never have realized that I've devoted my life to a unique and easy-to-follow diet and exercise plan:

The Body Minimal

The secret to The Body Minimal plan is *Minimal*. Remember that! Choice causes stress and anxiety and, therefore, overeating and exhaustion. Simply by following the Minimal food and exercise regimen, you eliminate decision making.

The Body Minimal is not a fad. It is a way of life. There are no pills, no powders, no yo-yo aftermaths—just a few Minimal daily suggestions.

MORNING

The morning meal *must* include rest and a newspaper. When you wake up, look at the clock and then pull the covers back over your head. This stretching action of pulling up the covers begins the daily exercise regimen.

After three or four good blanket-stretches, get up and wander around your house or apartment to the kitchen. Brew a cup of coffee, bend to reach for the newspaper that's been delivered to your door, and wander back into the bedroom. Wandering is safer than jogging in the park, and you can do it at any time in the privacy of your own home.

Feel free to have a croissant with butter and preserves for breakfast, but *never a pain au chocolat.* Chocolate for breakfast means unnecessary calories, and it might also leave a difficult stain in the bed.

Rest in the midmorning. This can be accomplished at home by never getting out of bed, or, with a few minor adjustments, in the office. Simply ask your office mates about their careers, personal lives, and any planned adulteries. Just by listening to gossip, you will take your mind off the passing Danish trolley.

An added tip for the morning: Always use a dial phone. Touchtone doesn't exercise the fingers and promote circulation like a good old-fashioned dial phone.

LUNCH

We now enter problem area number one: lunch.

Lunch is often anticipated as the highlight of the day until dinner. But why not skip it? Go shopping instead.

Especially good places to shop are malls or department stores with chocolate or cookie outlets. The calories burned by chewing and digesting truffles or macadamia chocolate-chunks while wandering through Calvin Klein size fours are considerable. Be careful, however, not to handle the sale merchandise without a napkin, as these items are not returnable.

Now, aren't you glad you didn't have the *pain au chocolat* for breakfast and worked off the sweets at lunch instead!

AFTERNOON

Teatime—time for a pick-me-up from the daily routine. Once more we are confronted with alternatives. Out comes the dreaded Danish trolley again. (Perhaps just one, to avoid another chat with the office mates.) Out comes the after-school Oreo treat. (If the kids can have it, shouldn't you demonstrate your affection by having one, too?) On comes "Another World." (Wouldn't the Frame family want you to share in their kaffeeklatsch while they discuss yesterday's marriage, bankruptcy, and teen-age fratricide?)

Teatime is precisely the time to think Minimal. Conflict is imposing itself, but the answer is simple: Teatime is the time to join a health club.

Be very clear about this! I am only saying to *join.* The effort expended in getting to the Club La Racquette and writing a check gives you a bonus of at least 200 calories that can be counted toward a late-night snack. And consider the investment of future calories you'll burn by opening your mailbox and carrying the weekly fliers for squash meets as well as the regular renewal notices. Followers of the Body Minimal plan have joined more than one thousand health clubs a year without ever having had to change out of their street clothes. It's fun, it's expensive, but it's never strenuous.

For variety, teatime is also a good time to join weight-loss programs, to buy hardcover workout plans, or to rent exercise videos at your local video shop. Carrying workout books and videocassettes can tone muscles as efficiently as jogging with weights. Again, I must emphasize that it is the effort involved in the preliminary exploration that is the most challenging and physically stimulating. The follow-through is routine.

DINNER

After a vigorous day of resting, doing dial-phone isometrics, and writing checks to health clubs comes your reward—dinner.

Now, I said the plan is Minimal; I never said it doesn't involve discipline. Just at the dinner hour comes the day's most stringent requirement: You *must* take a taxi to dinner.

Finding a taxi at rush hour involves leaping across the street, signaling rhythmically with an extended arm, and facing a hostile contretemps with fellow Body Minimalists. This is aerobics—pressing the heart to its limits! Moreover, the taxi ride itself will inevitably involve jolts over potholes, the irritation of a confused destination, and even a conversation in a foreign language. Riding the bus, taking the subway, or walking could never provide this much physical exertion.

At dinner, be sure to fill up on hors d'oeuvres and cocktails. This will leave little room for the main course. Besides, the natural oil found in the martini olive will help to replenish the skin. When dining out, you should scour the restaurant's menu for dishes unappealing to your particular palate. This way you'll be certain to leave a healthy portion of the meal on your plate. For example, vegetarians on the Body Minimal plan might enjoy a night out at Gallagher's Steak House.

We've arrived at the point where neophyte Minimalists often say: "This was Minimal so far, but what do I do about dessert? Do I get my 200-calorie bonus now?" The Body Minimal is a health and diet plan, and, as in any other health and diet plan, the secret to dessert is: *Think fruit.* Lemon mousse has fewer calories than chocolate mousse. Apple pie has fewer calories than Boston cream pie. Strawberry sundaes have a higher water content than hot fudge sundaes—and water is vital to fitness. The Body Minimal is at all times a *total* fitness regimen.

EVENING

After-dinner snacking is an inalienable right. Eminent physicians and miniseries stars have suggested various Band-Aid solutions—snacking on carrots, sunflower seeds, and unbuttered, unsalted popcorn, for example. Anyone who has tried snacking on carrots, sunflower seeds, and unbuttered, unsalted popcorn suggests leaving the house.

Leaving the house, however, can lead us into temptation. At the movies: buttered, salted popcorn and ice-cream bonbons. At baseball games: hot dogs and Cracker Jacks. At Broadway shows: sugary orange drinks and three-pound Chunky bars.

But science marches on. A growing number of Body Minimalists have discovered an anti-snacking breakthrough. When they opt to leave the house, they attend the noncommercial theater. The concession stand at a good Off-Off-Broadway play or New Wave dance concert serves granola cookies, bananas, black coffee, and cider.

The cost is usually $1.50 to $3.00 per item—and don't forget that contributions to the arts are tax-deductible!

NIGHTTIME

The day is almost ended, but desire knows no timetable. In the wee hours comes the constant refrain, "Don't I deserve a reward, a treat, a consolation prize for all my discipline and willpower?" Mrs. Marvin Finn of Englewood Cliffs, New Jersey, writes: "It's midnight—when do I get my bonus? What if I just split a little something with my husband? It's not his fault I had to modify my behavior. Don't I get to relax?"

Mrs. Finn, you do get to relax. Take a bath. And be sure to use nondigestible hair and skin products. Body Minimalists have saved thousands of calories by avoiding shampoos that contain avocado, beer, or honey.

Never go to sleep on a full stomach. If it's bedtime and you're still digesting, try watching TV to stay awake. Late-night television also offers challenging local slimnastics programs. Just changing the channel manually, instead of lounging with a remote control, tones the thigh muscles. And this is an activity you can share by alternating with your partner.

ADDITIONAL

The Body Minimal is the only minimal program that can change your life. To enroll in your FREE introductory session, call 24 hours a day, 7 days a week: 1–800–MINIMAL. Or mail this essay.

Warning: Consult a physician before beginning any dietary plan. The Surgeon General has determined that The Body Minimal may be hazardous to your health.

Tokyo Story

The most popular musical in Tokyo's history was *Fiddler on the Roof*. To many people, this would be a passing piece of theatrical trivia, but to a New York playwright in Tokyo to see her own play, it's a fact worth holding on to.

I've come to Tokyo for the final performance of my play *Isn't It Romantic*. The play follows the lives and loves of two young career women in modern midtown Manhattan. Much of its comic banter is related to such venerable metropolitan institutions as The Four Brothers coffee shop's breakfast special, Paul Stuart men in Paul Stuart suits, and mothers who sing "Sunrise, Sunset" every morning on their daughters' answering machines in the hope that it will encourage the young women to grab a suitable kidney specialist and march him down the aisle of the Carlyle Hotel. (The Pierre or the Plaza would do very nicely, too.)

Though my play ran successfully in New York and Beverly Hills, the specific references have rendered it "too New York" for most international producers. So my anticipation of this Ginza production is spiked by curiosity. I just can't imagine it!

"What is your play about?" my guide from the Tourist Information Center asks as we approach the Meiji Shrine on the first day of my visit.

"Oh, single women and their mothers." A Shinto priest wearing purple clogs bangs a drum for worship as I talk about New York women and their biological clocks.

My guide, Miss Tanaka, has a degree from Fordham University in New York. "You know," she whispers to me, "here a woman who is not married by age twenty-five is considered a Christmas cake after Christmas."

That evening, I decide to eat dinner alone in the traditional Nadaman Restaurant in the Imperial Hotel. This is a harder decision to make than it sounds because the Imperial has at least fourteen restaurants, including the rooftop Fontainebleau, where every night of my stay a chef from Williamsburg, Virginia, is celebrating the Fourth of July. All during my meal I can't help wondering what the other diners make of a woman ten years past the "Christmas cake" cutoff eating *futomaki* alone.

A *gaijin* (foreigner) friend who lives in Tokyo has told me the key to this city is that it's modern but not necessarily Western. To me everything—the neon, the crowds of people, even the subway—seems simultaneously alien and startlingly familiar. In the hope of coming to understand this tension, I plan to spend the weekend making a theater tour of Tokyo before seeing my own show. For a playwright, the theater is the most direct route into a culture.

The word on the street is that the Kabuki is in trouble. Of course, the word on the street in London is that the Royal Shakespeare Company is on the verge of bankruptcy and the talk of Broadway is that American playwrights have moved en masse to Los Angeles to write for "thirtysomething" and "L.A. Law." But the fact is that when the four-hour matinee begins at 11 a.m., the Kabuki is jammed. The audience is mostly women and mostly in pumps. (I later learn that theater audiences in Tokyo are generally 80 percent women. Going to see a play is apparently the ladies' cultural equivalent to the Boys' Night Out geisha evening. I gain no further insights into footwear.)

Although Japanese audiences are notoriously reticent, there is an audible gasp when Koshiro Matsumoto appears onstage at the helm of a full-scale eighteenth-century Nagasaki smuggler's ship that makes a complete 180-degree turn. It is simple, elegant, and altogether remarkable. I don't understand a word of the narrative, of course.

At intermission my matinee companion, Martyn Naylor, a Tokyo theater agent, takes me backstage to the leading man's dressing room. While Matsumoto, who is forty-four years old and strikingly handsome, swigs a hot purplish potion for his sore throat, my companion tries to persuade him to accept a part as a septuagenarian in an upcoming production of Herb Gardner's play *I'm Not Rappaport.*

"I don't think I want to play old again. It's just not right for my career." The actor flashes a winning smile. I have seen similar smiles in similar dressing rooms in London, Los Angeles, and New York. Even the purplish potion is standard.

Later, as we leave the theater, Naylor's enthusiasm is still contagious. "You know, the Kabuki invented the turntable in the 1700s. It's really quite remarkable when you see the way it's used in our production of *Les Misérables.*"

Les Misérables in Tokyo is a great show. But this is hardly due entirely to the turntable. Prior to the rehearsals, Shiseido, the cosmetics conglomerate and funding producer, established an "Ecole Les Misérables." The entire cast attended twice daily, four times a week, from early August to mid-April. Mr. Yoshikuni Sato of Toho Productions explains the process quite simply. "We wanted an exact replica of the West End or Broadway production. We want to make our musicals here just as excellent and sophisticated as anywhere else." Today cars, tomorrow the musical.

Glitzy musical show biz is not, however, new to Japan. In fact, for an extraterrestrial, good old-fashioned costumes-and-lights extravaganza, a stop at the Takarazuka Troupe can't be beat. If the Kabuki is the boys' camp, then the Takarazuka is definitely the girls'. At any given moment there are a hundred women onstage: fifty wearing gowns with sequins and feathers and fifty wearing top hats and tails. The biggest stars are the ladies who play the gents. In the Takarazuka production of *Me and My Girl,* the leading lady would certainly be "Me" and not "My Girl."

On the day of my visit the program is a Romanov romance, *The White Horizon*. Miss Tomoe Takashiro plays Sabinin, the handsome slumlord who falls desperately in love with Elena, the daughter of the Marquis Prozorov. The two are star-crossed lovers in 1890s Imperial Russia, dancing and singing Japanese. After intermission, we are treated to *The Best of Rhapsody,* a variety potpourri in which Miss Takashiro appears wearing a costume that I'm sure must be a Guinness record-breaker for plumage on a man played by a woman.

When, after the show, I talk briefly with the manager of the troupe, he boasts that the Takarazuka is unusual because "it is the one place where you will see older actresses. In America, a forty-year-old actress is common, but not here."

"Are they married ladies?" I ask. I'm back to my own agenda.

"No." He smiles. "As soon as they marry, they must leave. All the women in the Takarazuka are pure."

After completing my Tokyo theater tour, it is no longer my play's New York setting that troubles me about seeing it produced here. No. Now I'm afraid that Janie Blumberg, the main character of *Isn't It Romantic,* a Bachelor Girl who turns down a marriage proposal from a nice Jewish doctor, will be misconstrued as preferring to remain pure.

The Hakuhinkan Theatre, home to *Little Shop of Horrors, Plenty,* and now *Isn't It Romantic,* is located on the eighth floor of a toy-shop building in the busy Ginza district. On Sunday, the day of the final performance, the streets are closed to traffic. This is not due to a stampede for tickets. Sunday is Tokyo's shopping day.

Throngs of consumers are advancing on the Mitsukoshi, Matsuya Ginza, and Takashimaya department stores.

Martyn Naylor, his assistant Noriko Mitsuka, and I make our way through the crowds into the theater lobby. The Hakuhinkan is an intimate 350-seat house comparable to Off-Broadway's Lucille Lortel Theater, London's Royal Court, or Le Petit Montparnasse in Paris. From my experience, it is in these small houses that the best new work is done. The Hakuhinkan feels like home.

The director, Jin Uyama, approaches us. He is the first man I've met who is not wearing a gray suit or the latest earth-tones-and-shoulder-pads from Issey Miyake. Uyama wears blue jeans and a T-shirt, the international uniform of unaffected creativity.

He smiles at me. "I am, how do you say, anxious."

Immediately I want to commiserate. "Oh, honey, why do you think I was watching golf on CNN in my hotel room at four o'clock this morning?" Instead, I smile back. "I am very happy you did this play." Noriko translates for me. The words roll off her tongue.

The houselights come down on a backdrop of the skyline of Manhattan. My newly acquired knowledge of Japanese theater suddenly gels as Tasha Blumberg, the dancing vegetarian Jewish mother, spins forward on, of course, a turntable. From Kabuki to Blumberg . . . I am beside myself. Tasha wears a mint-green running suit and holds a telephone. "Moshi moshi," she greets her daughter's answering machine. Then she breaks into "Sunrise, Sunset" in Japanese. On behalf of my eighth-grade teacher, Mrs. Abelman, whose rigid foreign policy was that wherever we travel we are all ambassadors, I repress my giggle. But I can't believe this is happening. I'm thrilled!

The two leading ladies appear. Mitsuki Jun, who

plays Janie Blumberg, is a former Takarazuka star and is probably in her late thirties. Not only is this the first time she has played a twenty-eight-year-old American woman, it is probably one of her first roles as a woman. The elegant Midori Kanazawa plays Janie's best friend, Harriet Cornwall, a Harvard M.B.A. WASP princess. The only words I can literally understand are nontranslatables like "Vassar" and *"kasha varnishkes"* (Yiddish for little bow-tie noodles with barley). But when Naoie Hayasaka enters as Dr. Marty Sterling, the kidney specialist from Mount Sinai, and Janie and Harriet's interest is noticeably piqued, the play gets the very same first house laugh that it did in New York. An eligible doctor can break the language barrier.

In the intermission I greet the director once again and shake his hand. "Oh, you're so talented. It's amazing. You managed to get the same laughs we got in New York." His hand rests awkwardly in mine. I have momentarily forgotten that during intermission we are back in his culture and out of the international territory of plays and art. I have forgotten that with the houselights up, I must thank him with a bow.

In the second act, the play shifts into a more serious gear. In a scene at The Four Seasons restaurant, Harriet asks her very successful corporate-executive mother whether she thinks it's possible to "have it all." Although both women onstage are costumed for *Vogue* layouts, I am struck by how simply and straightforwardly the scene is played. This production is not a replica learned by rote in eight months of school. Someone here has clearly understood my play.

In the final scene, Tasha and Simon Blumberg bring their Janie a mink coat—something for her to wear when she's pushing the baby carriage in a year or two. To their dismay, however, Janie informs them that she has broken up with her boyfriend the dream doctor, and pleads with them to learn to trust her a little bit. When Tasha asks Janie who will take care of her when Tasha herself is not around anymore, Janie takes her mother's hand and assures her, "I guess I will." In Tokyo, just as in New York, the mother and daughter finally embrace.

The ladies around me at the Hakuhinkan are snapping their purses open for Kleenex. And I don't know whether I'm weeping because they are or because every mother/daughter embrace is fraught with emotion. Of course, it could also be because this particular dancing Jewish mother was modeled largely on my own, and it seems, to me at least, that Lola Wasserstein is now not only speaking Japanese but moving an audience in Tokyo to tears.

As I leave my seat, Jin Uyama follows me. "Tears? Tears?" Here is another international theatrical truth. Directors want their laughs, their tears, and only then is it time to go home.

"Yes, tears, tears." I show him my matted handkerchief.

The director smiles, just a little. "I am a revolutionary. That's why I did this play."

Now, in New York, making this statement would be tantamount to saying, "I am a revolutionary and that's why I directed *Barefoot in the Park*." But Uyama knows that his production of *Isn't It Romantic* has made the desired impression on this audience—an audience from a world of pure Takarazuka girls and twenty-six-year-old aging Yule logs. In this matinee performance my play seems to have realized the potential of its comedy. Perhaps I had to travel this far to understand why I write.

* * *

In Tokyo the closing of a play is an organized event. Each member of the company and crew gets to say a little something. At the *Isn't It Romantic* party, the speeches are mostly brief expressions of gratitude. The Hakuhin-kan producer, Nobuhiro Matsumoto, proclaims that he would like to do it all again. (Plays produced in Tokyo generally run for about a month; if successful, they subsequently tour Japan and are brought back to Tokyo the following year.) He then invites us all to help ourselves to a buffet of sushi, peanuts, French pastry, and beer.

Many of the actors seem too shy to approach me, but Midori Kanazawa (Harriet) comes right over. Through my translator she tells me that at first she did not understand my play and had to work very hard. But now, she says, she would welcome the chance to perform in another play of mine.

The party breaks into clusters. I see Mitsuki Jun (Janie) pulling the director onto a raised platform. He is shaking his head no and she is nodding her head yes. Blushing, he begins singing "O Sole Mio." I've certainly been to this part of the party before. It's a little bit of Bohemia by the Pacific.

The American theater has no official ritual to mark the closing of a play. There's a party, the set is struck, but there's no marking, no passage. In Tokyo the end punctuation on a play is a final *san-bon jime,* or clapping ceremony. I am asked to lead it.

Following Noriko's example, I clap three times, pause, then three, again three, then one more. I repeat the clapping sequence once, and *Isn't It Romantic* is closed, for now, in Tokyo.

As I head toward the elevator, Mitsuki Jun walks up behind me and extends her hand. She speaks English.

"Are you single?" she asks.

"Yes." I giggle.

"I thought so. Me, too," she says. "I am Janie Blumberg. She is mine."

It gives me extraordinary pleasure to think that I share Janie Blumberg with Mitsuki Jun, the former Takarazuka star in Tokyo.

Nails: The Naked and the Red

I knew my friend Patti was a big-time Hollywood agent the first time I saw her dial a telephone with a pencil. It wasn't that the pencil helped her get Streisand on the phone any quicker. No, it was the realization that Streisand and my friend Patti had something precious—something to love, honor, and protect from chipping—in common: their nails.

In a recent *Los Angeles* magazine Guide to Health, Beauty, and Fitness (I trust the city of Los Angeles implicitly in these matters), there are twenty-three nail-care salons listed. The Nail Patch in Encino offers complete care "that stresses the health of the nail." The services at San Marino's She Does Nails include "Juliettes ($20), Manicures ($13), Sculptured Nails ($45), and a set of even tips ($45)." I have no hard evidence of what goes on at Naughty Nails in Manhattan Beach. But I can dream, can't I?

Patti won't give away whether or not she uses modern nail technology to maintain her length. As with Streisand, only her naildresser knows for sure. But Patti does concede that there is a noticeable nail hierarchy in Los Angeles. Only the pampered housewives of Beverly Hills have the time and space to grow their nails naturally. Women under stress—studio executives, movie agents, stars of "The Young and the Restless"—rely on linen wraps and acrylic tips to maintain their digital contours. Secretaries and receptionists go in for frequent applications and color coordination with their clothes. As far as I can make out, the few remaining nail biters on the Coast are Hollywood writers unable to control their neuroses or their subsidiary rights.

Like the roaming, free-range chicken and the avocado before her, pampered nails have worked their way East. In truth, they've always been here, even when we weren't focusing on them. For temptresses from Shanghai Lil to Gilda, a tapered set of claws has been standard equipment. And I remember my high school gym-and-hygiene teacher advising us that a manicure is an essential part of good grooming. (This is the same woman who advised us against riding crosstown buses alone with boys from the Trinity School. Perhaps if I had not been quite so rebellious I would have grown up to be a temptress instead of a bus rider.)

It is also true that most of the grown-up ladies at the Bar Mitzvahs, weddings, and holiday celebrations I attended in my childhood always had their hair and nails "done." "Done" meant that neither food nor dance nor endless embraces nor cheek-pinching could muss or ruffle a thing. "Done" was a version of varnished. But I refer now exclusively to the grown-up ladies. We who cared only about giving peace a chance would certainly never care about our cuticles. In a better world cuticles would be irrelevant!

Well, we are the people we warned our parents about. There may not be peace, but, all the same, manicures have been liberated from being just something to do under the dryer. Nail care in New York has emerged from the shadow of the hair salons into a specialized arena all its own. There are now nail boutiques on practically every other street corner in Manhattan. At lunchtime on Wall Street, at afternoon-nap time on the Upper West Side, women from varied professions with varied dress codes take an hour to choose between a square and a round shape, linen or silk wraps for breaks, and—finally —pink, red, or green gloss. There's no denying that it's cheaper than a bottle of Obsession and less strenuous than aerobics. Sitting and soaking one's paws is extremely low-impact.

OK. Fine. And manicures are less caloric than a quick pick-me-up at Mrs. Fields cookies—she, incidentally, has terrific nails. (I checked them out when she was on "60 Minutes.") And, of course, nails can do so much for jewelry. Harry Winston has always appreciated good grooming.

But are well-buffed nails the hallmark of post-feminism? Do they signal that even though a woman runs a multimillion-dollar cookie business, she's still just a girl if her nails are pink? Or are manicures all about survival of the cattiest and clawing one's way to the middle? Honestly, I can't believe I'm thinking about this at all. But after I passed what seemed the tenth "Grand Opening" of a nail shoppe in the Thirty-fourth Street area the other day, I began to develop some theories.

To begin with, manicures involve never looking in the mirror. So the difficulty of beauty parlors—staring at yourself for two hours—is eliminated. Moreover, if you have to focus on one part of the body, the fingernail is a fantastic choice. Seldom does a nail have cellulite. It is also a lot easier to grow a nail than to follow the eight twice-daily steps of a total skin regimen. In dire, stubby straits, a facelift for the nails—a complete set of new tips —takes about an hour, and there's very little chance of getting involved in a prolonged malpractice suit.

And then there's the luxury. Now any girl can have her very own handmaiden without the lifetime beauty commitment of Helen of Troy or Helena of Rubinstein. Generally, a uniformed and discreet Korean or Rumanian woman chats about your cuticle shape, massages your hands, and with professional acumen coordinates your skin tone with the proper selection from the nail-color carousel. Unlike the facial ladies, who canvas pores with a magnifying glass and pucker at every blackhead, and the testy hairdressers who not very subtly inquire as to where you got your last haircut, manicurists never insult nails in their present condition—although they do suggest strongly, while applying the second coat, that you come in at least once a week.

Finally, the price is right. The cost of a manicure in New York City ranges from $18 at Bergdorf's to $7 at the local clip-and-polish joint. If, however, you care to eavesdrop on what everyone will be wearing to this week's benefit parties in honor of Henry Kissinger, Barbara Walters, and the Costume Institute at the Metropolitan Museum of Art, drop into the Thomas Morrissey Salon on Madison Avenue. (It's *the* "new" place, as opposed to Kenneth's, *the* "old" place.) It really doesn't cost much to rub cuticles, so to speak, with the Best Dressed List types, and you don't even really have to get dressed up. On the other (less intimidating) hand, if you're feeling a little blue and the world seems a nasty place, for $7 you can at least have rosy fingers.

The truth is that in order to write this piece I went to Barneys department store and had a manicure. (I've always favored the Stanislavski school of writing. Thank heaven this piece wasn't about facelifts.) Now, as I type, I like seeing the bright pink shadows bounce off the keys. And even though at this very moment I am sitting at my desk wearing a terry cloth robe, in my heart and on my fingertips I am well groomed and ready to shake any outstretched hand.

One last thought, and then back to giving peace a chance. I draw the line at French manicures—clear polish with white tips. I realize it's a rigorous struggle to maintain such a look, but I have little sympathy. And as far as French manicures accented with white moons are concerned, they are strictly the province of Imelda Marcos and the white-nailed Celonese sloth bear, who, by the way, has the best set of talons I've ever seen on a girl. In fact, I think contrary to the *Los Angeles* Guide to Health, Beauty, and Fitness, the best nail salon in southern California may well be at the San Diego Zoo.

Aunt Florence's Bar Mitzvah

A funny thing happened on the way to Aunt Florence's Bar Mitzvah. Actually, it was her grandson Gregory's Bar Mitzvah—Gregory is my cousin Rita's son—but I promised my aunt Florence, Rita's mother, that I would write about "her" Bar Mitzvah.

I'll get to the funny thing in a minute.

First, a word about Aunt Florence. She holds a special place in my childhood memories. On quiet afternoons at my family's house in Brooklyn, when my brother, Bruce, would be taking my sister for a mop ride and plotting openly to boil my blubber for oil like Moby Dick's, Aunt Florence would casually ring up to say hello and to inform us that "guess what," her son, our cousin Alan, had just finished reading and memorizing the *Encyclopaedia Britannica.*

"That's wonderful, Florence! Did he enjoy it?" My mother would always do her best to sound enthusiastic.

By this point my sister would have severed a few ligaments on the mop ride and I would be wailing that I didn't want my blubber boiled. My mother would approach us with the unchained wrath of Medea. "You goddamned kids! Your cousin Alan just finished the *Encyclopaedia Britannica,* and what the hell are you doing?"

In a rare moment of sibling solidarity we would answer: "Mother, nobody reads the *Encyclopaedia Britannica!*"

So Aunt Florence loomed large as a standard-bearer for elementary education in the 1950s.

But back to Florence's Bar Mitzvah.

When you reach a certain point in life, you stop doing all you can to avoid family functions and instead simply agree to attend. So there I am, driving to the Larchmont Temple. I'm wearing my a-little-dumpy, a-little-tasteful, a-little-clingy silk suit. Actually, it's a nice-girl family-function uniform, an updated version of the velvet crinoline ensemble complete with satin sash and matching ponytail bow. I get off the New England Thruway and remove from my purse the directions that my father made me promise three times I would write down: "Stop at two stop signs, make a right, go for one mile. Turn right onto the Boston Post Road."

As I cruise through suburban Larchmont, my mind is wandering all over the place. I want to know who makes dinner every night in these houses. Does the entire family eat together? Do they enjoy Lean Cuisine in front of the TV? Does the housekeeper prepare a pot roast and vegetables? And do they all show up for *their* family functions? I start giggling as I recall my favorite family-gathering story. It's the one about my friend Cindy's aunt Minah, who fell through the floor at her daughter's wedding. The Alley Cat got the better of her.

I turn onto the Boston Post Road. I'm wondering whether I will appear drab to the next generation. Pleasant, respectable, but never as colorful as Minah. I'm happy that Rita's son, Gregory, has a mother who's an accomplished lawyer and an aunt who's a playwright; Rita and I never had those female role models. But I also wish that Gregory could have known, back when they were my age, the aunts and uncles who now constantly flash pictures of their grandchildren. They were originals.

The living rooms of the members of my generation aren't draped in plastic to conserve the aqua lampshades and matching Louis Katorsky "The King of Home Furnishings" sofas. And when we throw parties we don't dial the number for chopped-liver sculptures. We prefer endive and radicchio salad with goat cheese en croute. Which is fine. Which is pleasant. Which is so tastefully assimilated. Which is why Aunt Florence urged Alan to read the *Encyclopaedia Britannica* to begin with.

Right now I just want to get to this temple. I want to stop thinking about what everyone in the town of Larchmont is watching on television and about my own life choices. I want to see my dad and my uncles in their yarmulkes. I want to stop resenting myself for being a solo family unit. I want to see them all. They have to take me in. They have no choice. They are my family.

Larchmont is about to become Mamaroneck. There's

an arrow indicating the road to Scarsdale. Even *I* know that the Larchmont Temple's got to be in Larchmont. I must have turned the wrong way onto the Boston Post Road.

I wish I wore crystals. Maybe they would calm me down. Breathe. Breathe. I see a sign for the Larchmont Motel on the left. I will make a U-turn at the motel.

The signal flashes with irritating frequency. I wait for two Mercedes and a Toyota station wagon to pass, and I'm into the Larchmont Motel parking lot. Three black children are playing out in front. My liberal heart takes note: Isn't that nice! While I've been completely self-absorbed, Westchester has changed for the better.

But there's a problem. The parking lot is one-way and seems to be blocked off. Actually, there are two problems. When I shift into reverse, the car continues to move forward.

I stare through the windshield. Now I see twelve children—some without shoes, some trailing baseball bats—and two women hanging laundry on a clothesline. A red-haired, red-faced man holding a beer can slams the door of a rotting car. He spits when he sees me. I know this is not the Yankee Peddlar Inn. I don't think the man approaching my car, beer in hand, is a friend of my cousin Rita's from Smith.

I have no more time to think about life choices, confusions, or nice plastic-covered furniture. There's a welfare motel on the Boston Post Road in Larchmont, Westchester, up the road from Toyland and next door to the International House of Pancakes. The world has changed since Alan read the *Encyclopaedia Britannica*.

The man with the beer can hurls himself, belly first, over my car. I can see his stomach rising under his T-shirt. He's screaming so loudly the veins in his neck are pulsing. "One way! One way!" His entire face is red.

"Oh. Oh, I'm so sorry. I'm so sorry."

Please, God, help me reverse this car and I promise I'll attend Bar Mitzvah services every weekend for the rest of my life.

"Stupid bitch!" He kicks the front fender of my car.

I pull the lever to R, step on the gas, and go forward, directly into his car. I am doomed. My ass is grass. *"Baruch atah . . ."*

The children are all gathering now. This is an event to rival Saturday morning cartoons. My nemesis rubs the dirt off his fender to investigate the damage. God bless Mr. Toyota and God bless his bumpers. It's just a bruise. Just a scratch. It wipes right off with a soiled T-shirt. If he kills me now, he has no just cause, and I have witnesses.

"Stupid bitch! Stupid bitch! Stupid bitch!" He clearly likes these words.

Time to go. It's been lovely. I enjoyed the morning buffet, the snacks by the pool, all the fun people, and I'd love to stay longer but my mother's having a heart attack at the Larchmont Temple.

I career out and head up toward Scarsdale. I plan to wait at least ten minutes before I U-turn. My palms are sweating. I'm nauseated. I feel hot. I feel cold. I want more than anything to go home and get into bed. But I don't want to go home to my apartment in Manhattan. I want to go home to Flatbush, Brooklyn, 1958, when all you had to do was be a nice girl and everything else would fall into place. And if you got good grades, everything would fall into place even better.

I want to feel safe, protected. And I don't mean the safety of having a doorman, a Burns guard, or a state-of-the-art security system. I want to feel for just one moment the safety before sleep, when it seems all's right with the world.

But all isn't right with the world. Of course, it wasn't in 1958, either. Stupid bitch!

"Hear, O Israel. The Lord our God. The Lord is one."

Thank God—the Larchmont Temple. A five-year-old girl in a velvet dress with a satin sash and matching ponytail bow stands guard before the entrance.

"It's almost over. You're late," she scolds.

"I know, honey." I know exactly who this little girl will be in twenty years, and I don't ever want to serve on her committee.

I crack open the door to the house of worship. Little glasses of wine are being distributed. I wonder if there's any way I could get about six of them.

From the back of the room I see my uncle Teddy, smiling tenderly at his constant date, Mrs. Spitzberg. (He's been seeing this woman for at least five years, but the entire family still calls her Mrs. Spitzberg.) And there's my cousin Alan, book in hand—he's reading, naturally.

I accept one glass of wine and take my place in the last row. My parents haven't noticed me come into the room. From the back my father looks the same as he did at my brother Bruce's Bar Mitzvah more than twenty-five years ago: the salt-and-pepper hair, the quiet yarmulke, the conservative blue suit. In fact, my mother looks much the same, too. She has style and zip, and her head is going in every direction, searching for her no-good-rotten-tardy daughter.

Removed, sitting in the last row, I realize that I haven't visited this world in years. I also realize that I tend to think of the various elements of this life—temples, Bar Mitzvahs, my cousin reading—as if freeze-dried in my childhood. I've forgotten that it all continues whether I show up and whether I participate or not.

L'chayim. The service is over. *Good Shabbes.* I make my way toward my family. I leap in, anecdote-first. "You'll never believe what happened." I kiss my father, my mother. I giggle and turn to my brother. "Brucie, I was almost in an accident in the parking lot of a welfare motel. Did you read *The Bonfire of the Vanities*?"

"Chris, did you hear that?" My brother nudges his wife. "Wendy was at that welfare motel. That's the one that Greg's speech was about."

"That was some beautiful speech!" My mother is setting up a third-generation Olympics.

"Well, Bruce, I was there."

"I thought I told you to write down the directions," my father says, taking my hand. "Aren't you going to say hello to Aunt Bessie?"

After we pay our respects to Aunt Bessie, I walk with Bruce and his wife toward the stage. Actually, it's probably called something else, but to me it's a stage.

Finally, I get to meet the Bar Mitzvah boy. I'm not writing this part just for Aunt Florence's sake, because I'm sure that Aunt Florence will already have heard the details of my account of this day's events, just as I'm certain that Alan will somehow have already read this: Gregory is lovely. Self-possessed, articulate, a nice boy, a sweet boy, a smart boy—the works.

I tell him I went to college with his mother. He's polite but not particularly interested. I tell him I heard that his speech was great and that I make speeches sometimes, too, because I'm a playwright. He says, "Cool." We're definitely warming up now. I tell him I was lost and almost got into an accident at the Larchmont Motel.

"Oh," he says. "My speech mentioned that motel. I

don't think we can ignore the world around us. Stuff like that."

I smile at him and nod my head. "Yes, I know. Stuff like that." I kiss him on the forehead. *"Mazel tov."*

I'm sorry I couldn't have fallen through the floor for him while dancing the Alley Cat. I'd like to have given him something really special.

"Isn't he terrific!" My aunt Florence nearly tackles me. "You should write something about my Bar Mitzvah."

The return trip is uneventful. I put soft rock on the car radio to keep me company. I'm now in the "not too soft, not too hard" rock-music age category. As I drive back to Manhattan, I'm still thinking about families, choices, the world of our fathers, our mothers, the one we're creating for ourselves, the one Gregory will create for himself, and the Larchmont Motel. Stuff like that.

The Sleeping Beauty Syndrome

THE NEW AGONY OF SINGLE MEN

Everywhere he went nowadays—the office, the Racquet Club, a closing, the dressing room at Polo-Ralph Lauren, Indian dinner with a hometown friend—Mike Smith overheard the same anxious conversation. "Have you seen that survey? Do you really think we put it off too long? Edwin Schlossberg was already forty-two when he got married. Can you hear my clock ticking?" There didn't seem to be a single man left in New York who didn't have those green and yellow circles emblazoned on his subconscious.

Mike Smith had never dreamed that that circle graph would mean anything to him. Surely *he* would never suffer from Sleeping Beauty Syndrome. After all, Mike, at age thirty-five, was a successful corporate attorney and in great physical shape. Mike had always just assumed that he'd find a well-educated, attractive, nonthreatening, high-income-earning, loving significant other. No problem. It was the birthright of a guy like Mike simply to go about his business, and when the time was right there'd be a suitable princess sleeping in his forest.

Well, that was before Mike Smith became a demographic. That was before Mike Smith and every still-single man his age realized that their nonchalance might have misfired.

TEARS AND MORE TEARS

The fateful news was broken to Mike and his brothers on "Entertainment Tonight." While interviewing Warren Beatty, Mary Hart held up two circles: a green circle representing the available sleeping beauty princesses, and a yellow circle representing those single men who, like Mike, still naively intended, when they were good and ready, to kiss a sleeping princess and—presto— "You're the prince of my dreams . . . I do!" Forget it, Mike! As Mary Hart demonstrated, the intersection of the circles was slight, and, as a man's age increased, not even worth mentioning. For fifteen minutes Warren cried live on tape. Also pictured crying were David Letterman, Mayor Koch, and Peter Martins.

And the tears weren't limited to the East Coast. It was Father's Day in Minneapolis when Dr. Marvin Cohen heard the news. The significance of the holiday only compounded the doctor's dilemma. Having recently split up with a seventeen-year-old senior at Exeter, and before that with a thirty-three-year-old Nobel Prize winner and former Miss Universe who insisted on talking "children/family/commitment," Dr. Cohen was on the verge of having to pack his own suitcase. "I really started thinking about the reality of a lifetime spent attending the AMA convention alone," said Dr. Cohen, a world-famous Ear, Nose, and Throat man. Two nights later he took a number and waited on line to meet the one still-single woman left in Minneapolis. It was a long night. His number was 63.

If left to his own devices Frank Wai Woo, a Hollywood stockbroker, real estate agent, and exercise guru, can happily fill his days pursuing his triple threat. But the news of the circle graphs made a dent. "I always knew women became desperate at thirty, but I thought we men had it made, if we were rich and fit enough, until at least seventy," said Woo in a phone interview from his Malibu beachhouse gym. "This is really bad news. I mean, hey, I exercise, I make four times my age, I actually bought and read *The Satanic Verses*. Why the heck are they turning the tables on me now? This is really lousy news. A big downer."

SQUASH COACH CONTRIBUTES

The big downer started as an unassuming academic study. "Big Hands and Big Feet Don't Mean Big Unhappiness: Single Men and the Sleeping Beauty Syndrome" first appeared in the *Ball State Review*. The authors of the study, two Harvard undergraduates working in tandem with a Ball State squash coach, explained, "We were fulfilling a Phys. Ed. requirement. We didn't mean to make anybody unhappy."

But they did. They made lots of people very, very unhappy. The profiles, histo-ries, and statistics in their report prove conclusively, without a doubt, what has long been secretly feared but never before said out loud. The truth is that attractive, concerned, intelligent, well-paid single men in their mid-thirties—big men on the campus of life—will probably never have a mate, and they might never even have another date. College-educated men born in the mid-1950s who are still single today have a .0002 chance of marrying (.00015 in Oregon). By age thirty-five the odds drop to .00000000006 (.00000000003 in Oregon). Forty-year-old men are more likely to have a Pan Am 747 land on their head!

No wonder Warren was crying.

BEACH CONDOS FOR BACHELOR GIRLS

But what happened to the available women? According to the Ball State survey, Bachelor Girls in their thirties, the former glut on the marriage market, after years of hearing predictions for a lifetime of desperation, depression, and empty isolation, have accepted and embraced their former plight. Baby boomer women are now content buying condos alone at the beach, having artificial insemination, and going to Tom Cruise movies on Friday nights with their women friends. Bachelor Girls under thirty are also in scarce demand. They enjoy temporary happiness with older, wiser, wealthier men (e.g., the Exeter senior and Dr. Cohen) or with much younger tennis stars.

Comments such as the following from single men have become commonplace in psychiatrists' offices across the country:

"Why didn't they tell us earlier?"

"Nobody mentioned this in Soc Rel [Social Relations] at Williams."

"You mean all the women at the Paul Weiss Rifkind Annual Dance will be married or lesbians?"

"I've started volunteering to stay all night in E.R. Since I can't bear to spend time around my friends who are married and have children, I've become a workaholic."

"Who will mother my children and pick me up from the dentist when I have my wisdom teeth removed?"

"I don't care that I'm worth 6.7 million dollars. My work and life are meaningless."

And it's going to get worse. Men in their mid-thirties must inevitably come face to face with their internal seismotic clock. Although for most baby boom professional men feelings of self-worth are derived from work and sports, every time there is an earthquake in Mexico, California, or Connecticut millions of men wonder "Who will hold me?" and "What use are my Mercedes and my second home south of the highway if they can all turn to ashes just like that?"

TURKEY BASTERS USELESS

Ironically, the Sleeping Beauty study's real message —that, by putting off marriage, seemingly eligible men have sealed their doom as "Uncle Harry who never married"—comes at a time of great prosperity. Restaurants now serving cholesterol-free pizza and grilled swordfish make it possible for successful men to delude themselves that they no longer need a little lady in the kitchen. But in their private moments, the pain of being single is overwhelming. According to Peter Quinn, a dry cleaner in Asheville, North Carolina, "At least women *plan* to marry. They scheme and prepare and talk about it with their friends. So if it doesn't happen, they've thought about that, too. But when a man doesn't marry, it's a real killer, 'cause he always just assumed he would."

The agony is most gripping for men in their thirties who want children. "There's nothing we can do with a turkey baster," said Dr. Fred Strommel, a weatherman in Cleveland.

"Everybody's having kids, and in *People* magazine Robin Williams and Chevy Chase are always carrying their offspring on their heads. If a woman carries her kid on her head, she's doing her job. But if a man carries a kid on his head, he's a nice guy. And I want to be a nice guy," confessed Hart Santore, an ex-philandering insurance agent in Tacoma, Washington.

"Everyone envies me, but I cry when I pass a nursery school," an unidentified source added.

There are some rays of hope, however. The survey points out that men born after 1970 may not have such a bleak outlook if they enter college and succeed in bestowing their M.R.S. degree before graduation. And for those born before 1970, there are support groups forming to help cope with life without "a better half." In Atlanta, for instance, men get together at Tiffany's every Thursday night and practice the art of thank-you note writing.

Dr. Ray Bismark, geologist and author of *Up Against the Seismotic Clock,* claims that, for the rugged, there are still ways to meet available women. "If you lose weight, cap your teeth, color your hair, and join a gym, video dating is a viable way to meet Mrs. Right. Also Personal Ads, Box 420009, *The New York Review of Books,* is one way to say, I'm out here, I've been hurt, I've been selfish, but I'm looking for a way to change." Dr. Bismark counsels to be creative. "For instance, artificial insemination waiting rooms and white sales could replace discos and clubs as 'in' meeting spots."

Finally, Dr. Bismark advises men not to be afraid to turn to their families in this emergency. "When Dad calls to say, 'When am I going to see a grandson?', don't hang up feeling like a pathetic, empty failure. Men should ask their fathers to help them out. Tell him everyone you meet is either married or gay, and you'd like to meet someone who has, say, an M.B.A. from Harvard but who still enjoys broiling lamb chops. If your father says he met such a girl on a plane, get her

number. And if she's great, then share her with a friend! 'Women Sharing' is a new and timely concept—there just aren't enough to go around." At present, Dr. Bismark himself is sharing the woman he adores with five other desperate bachelors.

LAVALIERING REDUX

This is a time for reevaluation and some great personal upheaval among baby boom men. If the result of delaying marriage has ultimately been the obliteration of the prospect of marriage, then is it too late to return to the old system of fraternity pinning, lavaliering, and engagement by junior year? But why glut the market at twenty? And, anyway, would it work? By the age of twenty women are already thinking about self-actualization and a year abroad. (It's those years abroad that lead to singles condos on the beach.)

Many geologists, anthropologists, and gym teachers are suggesting a return to the arranged marriage. If everything is settled at age seven, then there will be no reason for any adult to feel empty or depressed. With a contracted prince and a preassigned sleeping beauty for him to wake up in the forest, men and women will be free to concentrate on the important things in life.

WENDY WASSERSTEIN;
Tacoma, Asheville,
New York, Minneapolis,
Los Angeles

Modern Maturity

When I was in high school I was convinced that there was a simple rite of passage to becoming a grown-up. All I had to do was go see *A Man and a Woman* alone at the Paris Cinema. That is, at the Paris Cinema across from the Plaza Hotel in New York City.

The expedition was very carefully planned. My choice of film signaled that I was ready to move beyond proms and tailgate parties. (Not that I was all too frequently invited to either.) While foolish cheerleader types dreamed of football heroes, I envisioned my own true love as a French race-car driver/stuntman. Moreover, appearing unchaperoned on line for the 8:40 show made apparent to all innocent bystanders that I was so mature, so sensitive, so grown-up that I, like Greta Garbo, could actually prefer to "be alone." Finally, the Paris Cinema, simply by virtue of being a cinema that served demitasse in the lounge, as opposed to a movie theater that dispensed popcorn in the lobby, was second only in sophistication to Paris itself.

Of course *A Man and a Woman* is to this day one of the top-grossing films ever to be shown at the Paris Cinema. Thousands of fourteen-year-olds from Larchmont, Hewlett Bay Harbor, and the Plains of Jamaica made the pilgrimage, sucking in their cheeks and wearing sheepskin coats in the hope of looking more like Anouk Aimee. Maybe not all of them went alone. But I'm sure I wasn't the only one humming "Ba-ba-da-ba-da" and telling myself that what I was humming was French.

The struggle to be considered a grown-up begins, I believe, shortly after birth. Even a two-month-old can easily figure out that older siblings are allowed to stay up later, watch more television, and are the first in line for single rooms. Furthermore, children who don't engage in food fights, length-of-tongue contests, and excessive whining are generally rewarded with a seat at the grown-ups' table. It takes years, sometimes even decades, for most of us to become aware that the food and the conversation were, in fact, better at the children's table.

Being an early grown-up can have redeeming cultural value. I distinctly remember a class trip to the Metropolitan Opera for a special all-city elementary-school performance of Gounod's *Roméo et Juliette.* (By which I mean that the audience was made up of elementary-school students; the adults still got to sing and wear the costumes.) Our chaperon, Mrs. Philip Gordis, Susan Gordis's mother, cautioned us to behave like ladies and gentlemen so that we would be invited back next year.

I sat up straight, listened attentively, and thought how very impressed Juliet must be with my behavior. Yes, she was performing, but she was simultaneously thinking, "What a mature young lady in the third balcony!" Unfortunately, midway into the performance, a less well-behaved classmate of mine, a designated bad boy, shot a paper clip that nipped a rose from Juliet's crown as she trilled her wedding vows. Juliet immediately dropped her Romeo's hand and threatened not to continue until we all behaved. I was certain she didn't mean me, though. I knew I would be invited back.

By the time I got to college they had changed all the rules. Juliet probably ran off with my naughty classmate to perform impromptu paper-clip happenings in a meadow somewhere outside of Portland. Now the ideal grown-up was someone who never grew up. If "Don't trust anyone over thirty" was a credo, then forever remaining twenty-two—with long, flowing hair, macramé earrings, and Fred Braun sandals—was a life goal.

Those who got invited back were no longer considered mature—they were boring, establishment, and prematurely middle-aged. My new rite of passage to grown-uphood was hitchhiking to Yale in time for the strike (any strike) and really communicating with a disillusioned English major. A college friend of mine knew someone who knew someone who knew someone who spent the night with, or perhaps it was just some time with, someone who was the drummer or the something in Robbie Robertson's "The Band." Now *there,* clearly, was a grown-up!

* * *

It wasn't until a few years after college that I first associated being a grown-up with the accumulation of worldly possessions. Matriculating graduate students invariably brought with them cinder block bookshelves and a KLH system. A real J-O-B meant buying a real C-O-U-C-H. No more Indian madras bedspread coverups. No more hand-me-down fleur-de-lis loveseats from mother's "traditional" white-and-gilded collection. Workbench —and, for the professional trendy, Marimekko—was the hallmark of grown-up employment. A substantial piece of furniture costing between $300 and $700 proclaimed to the world, "No more teachers, no more books."

The couch investment was merely a harbinger of things to come. As I approached my "Gee, it's been great, but now it's time to settle down" late twenties, old friends from the frozen-pizza-for-dinner period began displaying serious culinary prowess and an interest in twenty-ton Le Creuset pots; the disillusioned English majors came to realize that they had always felt a pulsing desire to become interns in orthopedic surgery. Invitations to weddings in fields were rapidly replaced by traditional golf-and-field-club announcements.

They had changed the rules on me *again*. Within a year, being a grown-up required having a well-stocked refrigerator (sans red meat or preservatives), blue and white Royal Copenhagen plates, your own professional goals, a boyfriend (even better, a fiancé) with his own professional goals, a new, hipper, more expensive living space, and a blueprint for renovations. Only a child would insist on playing one round at a time and concentrating on a single set of rules and a single set of teammates. A grown-up could play forty rounds with forty balls all at once—and could make it look not only effortless but also like a hell of a lot of fun. Personally, I've always enjoyed a good solitary game of jacks.

Being a grown-up means assuming responsibility for yourself, for your children, and—here's the big curve—for your parents. In other words, you do get to stay up later, but you want to go to sleep earlier.

Maybe, as with other natural phenomena, the transition to becoming a grown-up is imperceptible. I recently went to dinner at the home of a married couple I know who are in their mid-fifties. When I arrived, my hosts and their friends were in the living room drinking scotch, debating the pros and cons of buying a house in Portugal, and updating each other on mutual friends' health and happiness. Meanwhile, in the study, the couple's college-age children were mixing blue margaritas, debating the pros and cons of film school, and updating each other on mutual friends' health and happiness. It was truly unclear to me with which group my allegiance lay. This became obvious, however, when the hosts' college-age son lifted the hors d'oeuvres tray and said, "Would you care for some pâté, *Miss* Wasserstein?" I decided to stick with the group old enough to call me Wendy.

So now that I'm official, at least chronologically, I'm not so sure it's everything I hoped for when I stood alone on line at the Paris Cinema. My ultimate desire from being a grown-up has never been a couch, a CD system, a lifetime supply of blue and white dinnerware, or three children who are fluent in French. (Nevertheless, I would not offhandedly reject any of these prospects.)

I suppose most of us imagine that one day we'll be sitting with an old friend, surrounded by their children and ours, and at a particular moment we'll look at each other and think, "This is it." Then the light will fall softly on our subtly streaked hair, our eyes will fill with loving tears, and the glow of happy days and fulfilled dreams will bloom on our Ivory girl—flawless skin.

Recently, I did visit an old friend who had just had her second child. As we sat trying to gossip while she fed her baby, and her two-year-old got caught in his rocking horse, and the collies came in for their rightful share of her attention, my friend made me swear that it wouldn't always be like this. To an untutored eye she was definitely a grown-up Mrs., and I was definitely a grown-up Miss. But the truth of the matter is that the next time my friend and I get together—when she returns to the city from her country house, gets a babysitter, goes back to work, and when I finish my overdue project, tackle the treadmill, and work on a relationship—we're planning to buy popcorn and champagne truffles, make silly drinks in coconut cups, and rent *A Man and a Woman* to watch on the new fleur-de-lis loveseat in my living room.

Reflections
on
Leather
Rhinos

My friend André loves too much. He is passionate, emotional, and obsessive —about ties. When he asked me one day to take him shopping for a suit, we started out with a specific itinerary: Bergdorf's, Saks, and Barneys. We set off with specific qualifications: versatility, day-into-evening convertibility, and a life expectancy of at least two seasons. And where did we land? Squinting over counters of numberless one-foot silks, comparing the specks of Missoni with the flecks of Armani and the good old stripes of Turnbull & Asser.

Male shoppers tend to stray. (I will refrain from commenting on how this tendency is reflected in other parts of their lives.) Department stores are particularly lethal. On nearly every occasion that I have agreed to accompany a pal on a winter-coat expedition, we have in the end returned home with two sweaters, an easy chair, a lap-top computer, and Bloomingdale's private-label decaf.

However, caveat emptor. If the men's department is located on the first floor, this straying can work in the co-shopper's interest. While you're saddled with his sport coat, his Irish knit, and his down jacket, there's a possibility that he will wander right into a Chanel counter or a display of Cartier tank watches.

In truth, I have never gone shopping with a man because I thought there might be something in it for me. I am a selfless, noble creature—well, not really. What I mean is, I have never gone shopping with a man because there might be something "material" in it for me. The attraction is the entry into a private world, a secret society. Is the boys' camp the same as the girls' camp? Or do they all slap one another on the back, with a hearty "Hey, guy, you look great. Let's eat some beef"?

My earliest memories of shopping with a man are of the annual trip to De Pinna with my dad to buy a blue cashmere coat. Every year he'd choose a version of that same coat, and every year, when he'd try it on, he'd turn to my mother and say, "Dear, what do you think?"

My dad belongs to a specific breed of male shopper: the loyalists. These true blues bought a sweater in 1952, and, by God, they've been devoted to that sweater, or to exact duplicates of it, ever since. Shopping with a loyalist is, for the most part, a soothing and secure venture. But it can get dicey when, as happens roughly once every ten years, he throws you a curve.

André, my friend with the tie compulsion, has been

wearing Brooks Brothers shirts since his prep-school days. One recent afternoon, approximately twenty years after his graduation from St. Paul's, I accompanied him as he purchased his annual stock of fifteen oxford button-downs, the heavier weight. Then, seized by a moment of wild-and-crazy abandon, he also purchased two striped Egyptian-cotton shirts without collar buttons.

Following this act of unrestrained depravity, poor André was troubled for at least three hours. But his anxiety was insignificant compared with my father's on the day De Pinna died. I mean, who else carried blue cashmere?

A distinction needs to be made here. Shopping with a loyalist is not the same as shopping with a traditionalist. A loyalist is anyone who has made his choice and sticks with it. So Sid Vicious in signature black leather was as much a loyalist as Antony Armstrong-Jones in his Burberrys trench. (Of course, Sid's kind of loyalty a girl would be better off doing without.)

The male shopper can be every bit as picky, finicky, and generally icky as his female counterpart. In my experience, it is the traditional dressers—the bankers, the lawyers, the corporate VPs—who are the fussiest. They can spend hours rejecting cuff lengths and lapel widths. And such prolonged deliberation can transform a perfectly helpful salesman with a tape measure into a caustic automated pincushion.

The difference between the selective male shopper and the selective female shopper is that the male seems to be much more surreptitious. For instance, my friend Parnell has a reputation for looking great in a sweater. He says he never thinks about it. He says he's shocked whenever people remark on his appearance. But I, who have shopped with Parnell, know that it is no coincidence that people take note of the way he wears a sweater. For Parnell, trying on a sweater is a ritual. He pushes the sleeves up and down, up and down, turning a cuff back over his wrist, crushing the wool at his forearms. Once the sleeve matter is settled, he attacks the issue of the waistband—should it be folded up or allowed to fall around the waist? The trick for Parnell is to accomplish his selection ritual without anyone's noticing. As soon as he sees that I'm entering the vicinity, he shrugs and says, "Yeah, I guess this one's okay. I don't really care."

Now I don't mean to pick on Parnell. There are plenty of others who are even more surreptitious. Some Wall Street investment bankers I know are so obsessively secretive about their shirts that they have started having them made by a tailor in Hong Kong rather than in nearby London.

And what about a bargain? Is "reduced" only a girl's secret best friend? The question is merely rhetorical after one trip to a showroom sale.

Twice a year my friend John and I hit the "not open to the public" (except it is), "by invitation only" (except it isn't) event at the Perry Ellis showroom. Inevitably the joint is jumping. Waiting lines only.

John has flying fingers. (He is a trained musician.) In minutes he can pull together a four-figure outfit—a shirt from basket A, a jacket from column B—for $150. The skill is all the more impressive since at showroom sales trying on is *verboten*. As John puts it, "You have to know exactly what you want." And John knows exactly. He is positively linenivorous. My mother, for all her "Honey, if they cut out the label, that means it's good" savvy, is an amateur by comparison.

I remember as a child rummaging through my father's wardrobe and finding the cardboard in his clean shirts the only item of any long-term interest. The giant leather shoes and the suits on wooden hangers seemed impossibly foreign. Even today, as a woman who's come to appreciate herringbone and hound's tooth tweeds, I still don't understand the appeal of Royall Lyme or stuffed leather rhinos, or have any idea why every traditionalist men's clothing store seems to carry both of them consistently.

The 1980s were a decade of carefully apportioned time-sharing as well as condoned conspicuous consumption —another red Adolfo suit for Nancy, another horse for Ron—and many American couples discovered that they could pursue life, liberty, a meaningful partnership, and a new pair of Nikes at the same time. This resulted in the popular phenomenon of Sunday his-and-her shopping. On a typical jaunt, a two-income couple with two hours to spend together before two separate engagements with two separate sets of old friends (he at a Pedro Almodovar film festival, she at a "Stocks for Jocks" seminar) find their way into pansexual, pan-vocational, pan-trendy emporia.

On Halsted Street in Chicago, Pioneer Square in Seattle, and West Broadway in New York, former dry cleaning establishments and envelope factories now converted into shopping spaces entice the "with-it"s to put their money where their good taste is. And it's all very low-key. The hair is inoffensively moussed. The music is Philip Glass.

In such spaces, I've seen duo-career couples commit to duo-equality by purchasing duo-guaranteed-to-wrinkle-shrink-and-impress-for-one-night-only aviator T-shirts. In such a space, I also fell in love with my friend Bill. On the verge of my thirty-fifth birthday, Bill and I decided to devote one Sunday to charging and being counted. By the time we entered our fourth dim loft space featuring row after row of parachute-weight earth tones, Bill shouted, "I can't find a damn thing in these places! And I can't see!" Bill has not strayed outside Charivari Sport, Banana Republic, and the Upper West Side ever since.

There are several reasons why I like shopping with men. Shopping with men allows me insight into character. Shopping with men allows me into those wood-paneled dressing rooms—a small step for womankind. Shopping with men allows me to express the kind of opinions about the opposite sex that they just assume they have a right to express about me and my wardrobe. I get to criticize their sleeve length, hips, thighs, and chest. Shopping with men allows me to participate, voyeuristically if not actually, in male bonding.

And now for the real reasons. Shopping with men means *I* don't have to try anything on. Shopping with men means some forgotten self-indulgence won't appear next month on my American Express bill. And, best of all, it means I get to go with them, or they get to go with me. Either way is fine. The possibilities are open.

My friend Christopher, a playwright, is a timid and tasteful shopper. He is also a shopper of fixed habits.

This is slightly different from being a loyalist. A loyalist could get quite finicky if a 300-count cotton weave were suddenly replaced by a 220-count. For Christopher, if the shirt fits, there's no reason to dither over eighty threads. Life is too short, and art too long.

However, Christopher does tend to return to the same shopping grounds: Constantine & Knight for shetland sweaters, Paul Stuart for blazers, and the Gap for corduroys. I have known Christopher for more than fifteen years, and in that time there have been two important accessory changes—a Harvard book bag that he carried for years and eventually replaced by a nylon shoulder bag, and a succession of various small winter ski hats that appear only on days when tundra conditions prevail.

A few years ago Christopher and I were in London together to appear on "Don't Miss Wax," a late-night talk show featuring Ruby Wax, a British cult heroine who grew up in Chicago, studied drama in Scotland, appeared for five years with the Royal Shakespeare Company, and is Great Britain's answer to David Letterman. In other words, if ever there was a time to wear all black Giorgio Armani with a Daffy Duck T-shirt, or a madras jacket and seersucker pants, it's when you're appearing as a guest on Ruby's show.

That afternoon Christopher and I discussed our wardrobes at length. Should we try to appear hip? Should we go to Covent Garden and outfit him in a Paul Smith linen duster? Should we tackle Burberrys so he could appear in a 400-pound raincoat? When we arrived at the studio where London's chic alternative late-night show is recorded, I was wearing a dotted dress and Christopher was in pants by the Gap, sweater by Constantine & Knight, and jacket by Paul Stuart. And Miss Ruby Wax, wearing a cowgirl skirt, boots, and a lasso, thought we looked just fine. Anyway, the other guest on the program that night was the rock star Meatloaf, and it would have been impossible to wrest the focus from his Hawaiian shirt, even if Christopher and I had come dressed as the Chrysler and Empire State buildings, respectively.

My very favorite shopping-with-men incident took place on an impromptu excursion with Christopher one recent winter afternoon. Neither of us was in the mood to brave the department stores, and Christopher didn't have enough mousse in his hair to deal with NoHo, SoHo, or HoHo. So we decided to check out Star Struck, a thrift shop in Greenwich Village. There we found, between the zoot suits and Elvis jackets, a blue cashmere coat.

I, who was trained to recognize quality goods, ventured the educated hunch that this coat had been born on a rack in De Pinna's. I held it up for Christopher and asked, "Dear, what do you think?"

Perfect Women Who Are Bearable

A friend of mine once rode in an elevator in California with Jessica Lange, Sam Shepard, the children, and the nurse. According to my friend, who is discerning in these matters, she's beautiful, he's beautiful, the Baryshnikov baby is beautiful, the Shepard babies are beautiful, and the nurse was very capable. I asked whether this elevator ride was part of a Lange-Shepard family trip to the Academy Awards. My friend replied, "No, they were just spending quality time together."

I have never met Jessica Lange, but I nonetheless have complicated feelings about her. I remember feeling encouraged by her performance in *King Kong*. If a pretty model would risk being filmed in a monster's claw to become a movie star, then maybe a "casually attired" New

York writer, like me, could one day become the spokes-person for Guess jeans. Jessica seemed to be pushing herself, extending her craft, changing her life for all of us. Go, Jess!

But somewhere around the time of *Tootsie* and *Sweet Dreams* things began to change. The Baryshnikov child came along, then the unpretentious cabin set among Minnesota lakes, the two Academy Award nominations, and domestic bliss with Sam Shepard in an alternative American family. OK, Jessica, I'm impressed. I take you seriously. You're a role model now. But there's no way that we could be friends anymore. And it's not just that I'm envious—which of course I am. It's that thinking of you makes it even more difficult to get out of bed in the morning.

Now, I know I probably shouldn't take Jessica quite so personally. Like I said, I've never met her. Still, there she is: a movie star, a feminine ideal. In the forties emu-lating an ideal woman meant bobbing your hair like Betty Grable's. In the eighties, because of Jessica, women have to get an Academy Award-nominated Pulitzer Prize-winning actor-playwright to fall in love with them, have a child by one of the world's great dancers, be nominated for two Academy Awards, and enjoy doing the laundry alone on a farm. Christ, I'd do anything just to have to bob my hair like Betty Grable's!

And it's not that I want to push the clock back to when "having it all" meant having a facial, shampoo, and manicure. In fact, I want to push it all forward a little. Look, maybe there *are* women in this world who simply crave bean sprouts, learn Italian from a cassette while driving to the law firm, raise children who watch only public television, have their secretary write thank-you notes after every social engagement, know what to say at a dinner party when they're seated between Michael Jackson and Senator Dole, and acknowledge their periods of self-doubt by taking a month alone to fish in Michigan. But my point is that there are also accomplished, civilized women, role models even, who don't make you think that no matter what you do, it's simply not enough. Girls don't just want to have fun. But certainly a lighter touch would sometimes help.

Since we are all at the mercy of life-style trendsetters who tell us when it's time to stop admiring Jane Fonda and to start focusing on the nonthreatening Vanna White, I propose an equally arbitrary list of bearable women. Or to put it more simply, women who make you *want* to get up in the morning.

Here goes:

1. Elizabeth Taylor. Anyone who can marry that many times, gain and lose that much weight, refer to Montgomery Clift as a friend, star in both *Who's Afraid of Virginia Woolf?* and *X, Y and Zee* is not only extremely bearable but has something to teach.
2. Chris Evert. She's so talented, yet entirely devoid of glitz or charisma. I can't imagine what Chris would say to Michael Jackson and Senator Dole.
3. Jane Goodall, who lives with chimpanzees in Africa. It would be helpful to talk with Jane about where to meet available men.
4. Heidi Landesman, winner of two Tony awards, one for Scene Design and one for Best Musical. Heidi, who is lithe and lovely, lives on candy corn and chocolate mint lentils. She has been known to leave rooms in order to avoid exposure to bean sprouts.

5. Jane Pauley, who had the good sense to be pregnant on national television. One appreciated Jane's controlled flares of caustic humor after Bryant Gumbel interviewed an astronaut, a prime minister, a golf champion, and Jane had a friendly chat with the man from South Dakota who invented a new broom. Jane also had the savvy to demand an alternative arrangement as soon as NBC's intentions for Deborah Norville became apparent. A lesser woman might have ripped Deborah's hair out.

6. Jacqueline Kennedy Onassis. She still goes to the theater, she helped save Grand Central, and she married her daughter off to a nice Jewish boy.

7. Ann Richards, a Texas politician capable of filling the boots of both Sam Houston and Lyndon B. Johnson. She's a tough-minded liberal and a good ol' gal. Ann quotes Mae West in her campaign speeches, and through it all she stands tall on legs to rival Betty Grable's.

8. Meryl Streep. She'll never pass you a poison apple. Meryl just goes about her business.

9. Molly Yard. President of NOW and an American classic—Georgia O'Keeffe, Emma Goldman, and Elizabeth Cady Stanton all rolled into one. Anyone who's considering a facelift should catch a glimpse of Molly. She's all character and she's just beautiful.

10. Mathilde Krim, a lady doctor married to a gentleman CEO. She could be one of the lunch crowd at Le Cirque, but instead devotes her time and talent to AIDS research. Mathilde wears Arnold Scaasi for a greater purpose.

I was not going to include a list of unbearable women because no women are unbearable. But these women come close:

1. Ivana Trump. I certainly would be upset if every building I passed was Wendy Parc or Wendy Tower. How does she figure out which one is home?

2. Patti Scialfa. It was bad enough when Bruce Springsteen married Julianne Phillips. But at least she was a nice girl. When he dumped her for a miniskirt in fishnet stockings, I lost all respect for him. He is no longer my Boss, and I blame it all on Patti.

3. Georgette Mosbacher. It is an unenviable title to be the glamour woman of the Bush era. But she's a natural at corporate tactics and home entertaining. And to quote Donald Trump, "That Georgette is some gorgeous woman!"

4. Marilyn Quayle. Dangerous Liaison.

5. Michelle Duvalier. Shopping is one thing, but Marie Antoinette syndrome is something else.

6. Erma Bombeck. She finds Jell-O molds and housekeeping so amusing.

7. Perri Klass. Featured in *People* magazine at age twenty-eight: an intern-novelist from Harvard Medical School with a preschooler and a house spouse-novelist-academic husband-equivalent. Enough said?

8. Fergie. She was terrific, a jolly hockey-sticks kind of gal, when she first arrived. But later she began taking the limelight away from poor shy Di and having too much of a ball with those fun-loving royals.

9. Diana Ross. Anyone who could behave that way to Flo and Mary is not supreme. And no wig or beaded dress will ever camouflage her true self.
10. Nancy Reagan. You *can* be too rich and too thin.

For those of you who disagree about Meryl Streep being bearable, I want you to concentrate for a moment on Midori, the teenage violinist, and one of the music world's most promising talents. At least Meryl is an eighties person, or a seventies person. Midori is a nineties person or, worse, a twenty-first-century person. And the thought of the complex balancing act that next-century women will be required to perform is enough to make anyone never want to get out of bed.

Among nineties women there are, happily, some bright prospects. Consider, for example, Martha Plimpton. Martha, who turned nineteen on her most recent birthday, has acted in films with Woody Allen, Judd Hirsch, and Robert De Niro. She's a committed Vegan— no meat for Martha—and she marches against fur and animal exploitation. The critics say her acting is subtle, funny, and real—and it's true. It's also true that Martha remains bearable: funny, scrawny, bright, articulate in talking about everything from her boyfriend to Allen Ginsberg's poetry.

So maybe on days when the perfection of Jessica looms so large it's slightly hard to function, take a deep breath, think of Martha, and blindly continue. Rome wasn't built in a day. And it would be unbearable to think that *you* could have done it any more quickly. Unless, of course, you were Georgette Mosbacher.

Big Brother

I slept on the floor of my brother's room during the Cuban missile crisis. It seemed to me that if "they" came—I wasn't even quite sure who "they" were: the Russians? the Cubans? both? —my brother, baseball bat in hand, would be there to protect me. At the time it didn't occur to me to question why "they" would want to come specifically to Brooklyn, to our house. I know only that in my mind's eye I saw them using my mother's washer-dryer in the basement and forcing us to watch *their* TV shows instead of our habitual Friday night lineup: "Rawhide," followed by "The Flintstones," with a late-night capper of "77 Sunset Strip." Looking back now, my fears seem like manifestations of early free-floating anxiety. But there was only one thing I felt certain of then: whatever happened, my big brother would be able to deal with it.

During my elementary school years my brother ranged from being this magical person who got to play basketball in the driveway right up until dinnertime to this irritant in a leather cap with earflaps who would knock on the window of my first-grade classroom for the sole purpose of sticking his tongue out. In a Grand Guignol gesture of revenge against my sister and me for having sprayed his face with shaving cream, my brother charged into our room, dumped all our clothes out of our dressers, and carved his initial *B* with his blade, a Magic Marker, on our pajamas, just as his hero of the moment, Zorro, carved a *Z*.

My brother and I spent a great deal of our formative years exploring. Where he went, I would go, too. It was a given. And it wasn't that I was a "tomboy" or that he and I didn't have our own separate worlds. I liked Ginny dolls and Broadway musicals; he liked chess and Landmark history books. Still, we were great friends.

I believe our filial attachment was based on an unspoken agreement—that whatever I said couldn't possibly be as brilliant and penetrating as his comments on the same subject. True, we never delved into his opinions on matters in my areas of expertise—the summer-camp production of *Peter Pan* or why Barbie was second-rate compared with Ginny. He did, however, take me places and solicit my opinion in worlds where Sandra Dee and Gidget were simply not expected to be.

Sometimes I wonder whether many of my current friendships with men aren't influenced by those years with him. Not that I've ever again latched onto anyone who wanted to carve a *B* onto my pajamas. But I derive great comfort from long-term friendships with men— brother figures actually. We don't play emotional games with each other, and I don't worry about whether they'll ever call me again. Nonetheless, I still fall into the trap of thinking, "Oh, he's brilliant, he's smarter than I'll ever be." And they no doubt get pleasure of a sort out of being around someone who feels this way.

Since our exploring days, my brother, Bruce, and I have followed entirely separate paths in life. He is a banker, a visionary in a world specifically built "for profit." I am a playwright; I work mostly at publicly funded institutional theaters specifically termed "not for profit." He has a lovely family. I live alone. In my brother's universe young men make millions, buy estates in Greenwich and East Hampton, and learn to eye Arabian horses. In my universe, a few young men and women make millions, but many live in one-room walk-up apartments.

The wives of my brother's friends are more than socially adequate. They are qualified experts. They know which decorator, caterer, doctor, nursery, even which friends are precisely the "right" ones to choose. It's an art, an accomplished skill. Some of these wives are doctors, attorneys, businesswomen; others are or will be prominent hostesses and chairpersons. I admire their ability, even their desire, to keep up with their social positions. I suspect that, on the other hand, to many of these women I seem an eternal bohemian, sheet-clad and frolicking on a lawn at Bennington College. What they haven't caught on to is that sometimes I wish I knew the "right" caterer, too. However, unlike them, I won't judge myself too harshly if I never do.

These many differences in our lives have come between my brother and me. We travel in orbits that rarely intersect, and in some ways we've become enigmas to each other. There's little I can say about my life that I think he will easily understand—I'm not making mega movie deals or marital deals, and I don't have a game plan, a strategy. His secretary still places his calls to me; when he gets on the speakerphone he inevitably bellows "What's new?" And I can't help wondering whether what I say has any relevance for him at all.

A few years ago, shortly before my brother's fortieth birthday, I won a grant to write and study theater in England. I had already been living in London for several weeks when one afternoon I received a message that my brother was in town and staying at the Ritz. (I myself was staying at the Nell Gwynn House in a one-room flat where overturned flowerpots were used to accent the green-bedspread decor.) I can hardly describe what my hosts, good Labourites all, thought when my brother's secretary explained to them that I was to call her in New York to make arrangements for my dinner with him in London.

I loved that evening with my brother. I loved running into a friend from New York at the restaurant and introducing my glamorous, mysterious dinner companion. I loved talking to Bruce about our parents, his wife, my marital prospects, and his extraordinary children.

At the end of the evening, around 2 a.m., we took a walk down New Bond Street. We just went walking, exploring. He didn't ask me, "What's new?" I didn't tell him that I thought calling his secretary in New York to make dinner arrangements in London was absolutely cuckoo. And happily, to our mutual surprise, we learned in time for my brother's fortieth birthday that we could again—still—be great friends.

She Ate Cake
with
Marie Antoinette

he first time I heard the name Vigée Le Brun, I assumed it belonged to a stripper. "Tonight the Versailles Room proudly presents . . . Miss Vigée Le Brun." I had no idea that Madame Le Brun was the favored painter of Marie Antoinette, and had completed more than 660 portraits in her lifetime.

The real Madame Elisabeth Louise Vigée Le Brun first became familiar to me when I began doing some art history research for my play *The Heidi Chronicles*. Dr. Heidi Holland, the play's eponymous heroine, is an art historian who describes herself as "neither a painter nor a casual observer, but a highly trained spectator." For specific reasons, I wanted Dr. Holland's field of primary interest to be women artists. What I had never imagined was that in my research I would discover a vast range of artists, Madame Le Brun among them, that my education and the education of most of my contemporaries simply ignored.

I can picture myself sitting in a classroom filled with intelligent young women at Mount Holyoke College in 1969, all of us carefully looking at the slides for our art history survey class, all of us dutifully taking notes, and none of us ever asking why no women artists were mentioned. And certainly our textbook, H. W. Janson's *History of Art*—"from the Dawn of History to the Present Day"—which has since become notorious for not mentioning a single woman artist until its third edition in 1985, did not prompt us to challenge the situation.

Therefore, when Thomas Lynch, the designer of *The Heidi Chronicles,* and Dan Sullivan, the director, suggested that a feminist protest scene at the Art Institute of Chicago be staged as coinciding with an "Age of Napoleon" exhibit, I accepted unoptimistically the task of identifying women artists who might have been excluded from the exhibition. Offhand I couldn't think of a single one. I had visions of pursuing the watercolors of Desiree, the film-version mistress of Marlon Brando's Napoleon. I never suspected I'd find not an obscure or fictional artist but a fine and serious painter. Now it gives me great pleasure whenever, in Act I, scene iv, at the Plymouth Theater, I hear "Elisabeth Vigée Le Brun" shouted out as the name of a woman artist ignored by this fictional exhibit. Vigée Le Brun may not have been a dancer, but she did make it to Broadway.

Her career was remarkable. Born in Paris in 1755 to a minor portrait painter and his peasant wife (a hairdresser), Elisabeth Vigée was essentially self-taught. To quote Madame Le Brun from her fascinating if somewhat self-serving memoirs (written when she was well past her prime), "my love for painting declared itself in my earliest youth." Sent to boarding school at age six, she "scrawled on everything at all seasons; my copy-books, and even my schoolmates', I decorated with marginal drawings of heads, some full-face, others in profile; on the walls of the dormitory I drew faces and landscapes with colored chalks." Later, she polished her skills by copying the Rubenses, Rembrandts, and Van Dycks in the gallery of the Luxembourg Palace. By her late teens, she was painting portraits and earning money at it.

After her marriage at twenty to Jean Baptiste Pierre Le Brun, a charming though happy-to-be-supported art dealer, Madame Le Brun became an established court painter. According to sources even other than herself, she was witty, charming, attractive, and a delight to have around. True to the fashion of the time, she flattered her subjects with likenesses that minimized their physical defects; but, more often than her contemporaries, she painted her subjects in natural, sometimes even occasionally suggestive, poses. Madame Le Brun's politics also fit her times; she was, to say the least, a royalist. If Marie Antoinette had ever told Madame Le Brun to "let them eat cake," Madame Le Brun would most likely have found the remark gracious and darling.

Madame Le Brun painted more than twenty portraits of Marie Antoinette and, to judge from the artist's memoirs, her own favorite of all her paintings was a large 1787 portrait in which the queen sits next to an empty crib and is surrounded by her three surviving children. (In recent years, pentimenti are beginning to show through the painting's surface to reveal the likeness of the baby who died before the painting was completed and had to be "erased" from the finished composition.) So it was to Madame Le Brun's horror that during the Age of Napoleon, which she spent in exile in Italy, Austria, Russia, and Germany, this painting was not only relegated to a corner in the Versailles palace but turned around, its face to the wall. Madame Le Brun had the last word, however. When the Restoration came, the painting was re-exhibited at the Salon. As for herself, Madame Le Brun retained for her own collection a portrait of Marie Antoinette ascending to heaven; "to her left, on some clouds, are Louis XVI and two angels, symbolizing the children she had lost," she wrote.

What fascinates me about Madame Le Brun is her day-to-day life as a working woman artist. Even after she was forced to flee Paris in 1789 following the invasion of Versailles, she continued to paint, setting up studios in St. Petersburg, Moscow, London, Vienna, and Naples. And in each situation she managed to flourish. Her subjects, wherever she went, included local royalty. Her memoirs are full of anecdotes about such diverse personal friends as Count Orlov, Catherine the Great, Byron, Prince Metternich, the Prince of Wales, and Poniatowski, "the last king of Poland and an amiable character."

Although in her memoirs Madame Le Brun portrays herself as a Lady of the Upper Classes who happens to paint, what slips through all the glitter and finery is her essential seriousness of purpose as an artist. When she arrived in London in 1802 she noted "that city affords less food for the artist's interest than Paris or the Italian towns," and was distraught because there was no "picture gallery" open to the public. "In default of pictures," she writes, "I went to look at the public edifices," returning to Westminster Abbey several times to study the tombs of kings, queens, and poets.

Also while in London, Madame Le Brun encountered Sir Joshua Reynolds, who came to see her portrait of Finance Minister M. de Calonne when it arrived from Paris. (This portrait had helped to destroy her reputation in Paris because rumors circulated in the press that she was having a love affair with Calonne.) She recounts the story of "some nincompoop" exclaiming in front of the picture, "That must be a fine portrait; Mme Le Brun was paid eighty thousand francs for it!" And Sir Joshua Reynolds replying, "I am sure I could not do it as well for a hundred thousand."

Studying Vigée Le Brun's self-portraits one begins to get a deeper sense of the artist as a lady of her times. In her self-portraits with a letter, 1782, with daughter, 1786 and 1789, and alone, 1790, we see her treat her own image in much the same way that she treated the images of her sitters. Her clothing is interestingly draped, adorned with a feather or light accessory, and there is a Rubenesque fluidity to the painting. Each of the self-portraits is charming, especially the compositions with her daughter. But in them the artist's countenance is neither regal nor frivolous. There is nothing "sweet" about this Madame Le Brun. She is not on clouds ascending to heaven. The face of the artist— though I'm sure she'd be appalled by this insinuation— is that of a working woman painter.

There is probably no woman further from a stripper than Elisabeth Vigée Le Brun. She was a self-supporting career woman who managed against all political odds to pursue her art. Looking at her prodigious work, and the consistently high quality of it, one begins to discard any notion that her success might have been due to her charm, her wit, or her social connections. Madame Le Brun was serious and very good. And though I'm sure she was the best of friends with the kings and queens of Poland, Russia, and France, my hunch is that they let her stay for more than tea because ultimately they too recognized that she was serious and very good.

A Screenwriter's Diary

January 1986: I have recently fallen into the 1980s bad habit of not returning phone calls. And it's not because I'm arrogant. Hardly. In fact, the opposite is true. I am one of those people all the self-help manuals are aimed at: "It's OK to Say No," or "Why Do My Lips Say Yes Yes Yes When There Is No No No in My Heart?" I am entirely capable of making five appointments for the same lunch, or agreeing to write five assignments due the same day. So this new habit of mine is self-protective.

But then I get this message that's tempting:

"Hey, Wen." (The "hey" means he's calling from California.) "This is Jon Denny. Phylis Geller suggested I call ya. I'm putting together a series of half-hour comic films for KCET [a California public television station]. Would love to see ya while I'm in New York."

I have a history with Phylis Geller and public television. Phylis, who is now vice president of national productions at KCET, was the producer of my play *Uncommon Women and Others* for PBS's "Theater in America" series. And although PBS never arranged to market Uncommon Women dolls, and I was unable to retire on my four-figure deal, there exists a televised version of my play shot from my own script and featuring a cast that includes Swoosie Kurtz, Alma Cuervo, Meryl Streep, Anna Levine, Josephine Nichols, Ellen Parker, Ann McDonough, and Jill Eikenberry in her prime-time debut as a high-powered lawyer. That kind of good experience is enough to make any writer pick up the phone.

February 1986: "Hey, Wen, this is Jon Denny, and I've been waiting for ya under this clock at the Marriott Marquis. I'm pretty sure our date was for today."

Here is the definite downside of making five appointments for the same time.

Nothing motivates a writer like guilt. Obsessed with a vision of this Jon Denny sipping coffee under the clock and calculating how many revolutions the Marriott bar makes around Broadway in an hour, I call his hotel, promise to buy him a co-op, and arrange for a rain check —tomorrow, same time, same place, no conflicts.

Jon Denny has enormous energy. Even for a man in his twenties whose official title is "Creator and Producer," his energy is surprising. I arrive at the Marriott, embarrassed and humiliated, and while still shaking hands he tells me how great it is to see me, we're going to do such a terrific show, everyone is thrilled. We get a cup of coffee from the buffet trolley, and I wonder whether this can be considered a power breakfast.

"So, Wen, what do you think?"

I think I'd like it if he would stop calling me Wen. His idea for a series is called "Trying Times," an oblique look at overcoming small contemporary life traumas. He hopes to enlist such writers as Jules Feiffer and Spalding Gray and to produce the first comedy series ever created for PBS.

"Wen, does it ring a bell?"

Thanks to my high school training as a panelist on the *Herald Tribune* World Youth Forum, I tend to offer an answer to a question when challenged. For ten points, I can come up with a small life trauma: I confess that, at age thirty-six, I have recently spent the better part of two years careening around Manhattan in a Taggart's student driver car. After two tries, I finally received my license, having appeared at the Bronx testing center at 8 a.m. wearing a black cocktail dress and pearls. The time I flunked—the first time, in Manhattan—I had shown up in blue jeans and a sweatshirt.

As I wind up my third student driver anecdote, Jon shakes his head. "Why don't you turn the driving instructor into a man? Try a little romance. Or maybe our heroine becomes obsessed with cars. Maybe she's an accountant who quits her job to be on 'The Dukes of Hazzard.' "

He hands me a cassette of an already produced episode of "Trying Times" written by Beth Henley.

"Wen, this is gonna be great."

I guess I've said yes.

March 1986: I watch Beth Henley's small life trauma video for inspiration. It is an original comedy directed by Jonathan Demme. There's a lot to be said for a small film featuring actors you'd really like to work with and based on a script that is not farmed out for rewrites. I decide to settle down and open up my dreaded Driver's Manual. Perhaps my teleplay will bring comfort to those who panic whenever they have to change lanes.

April 1986: Public television—glamour and high stakes all the way. Jon Denny and I have our first script conference at a Lenox Hill coffee shop.

"Wen, does a marching band have to break into 'Little Old Lady from Pasadena' when our heroine passes her test? And what about the tollbooth scene? This is public television and tollbooths are expensive. Does she have to get her anxiety attack at a tollbooth?"

Jon assures me we will get the actress Catherine Bach, who for years played Daisy, the hot-rodding ingenue on "The Dukes of Hazzard," to appear as her TV character in a cameo role in our show.

"Wen, I'm telling you Catherine Bach and you and I will be shooting in Edmonton this July."

I'm looking forward to summer in Canada.

May 1986: "Wen, want you to know everyone here is very excited about the second draft, and we're talking August in Toronto."

August 1986: "Wen, October in Vancouver."

October 1986: "Wen . . ." He calls me from the coast just as I'm feeling quite fond of all that energy. "I have some ideas for leading ladies. What do you think of Barbra Streisand or Bette Midler?"

Suddenly I mount a very high horse. "You want Barbra Streisand to play an emotionally repressed college professor who is afraid of motion? I didn't agree to work for public television to have this kind of conversation."

"Just tossing out names, I'm also thinking Teri Garr, Dianne Wiest, Swoosie Kurtz, Mary Beth Hurt."

Better. I can breathe.

November 24, 1986: Shooting is set to begin just after Thanksgiving. We have a commitment from Teri Garr, but we're still lacking one romantic lead/driving instructor.

"This is Sheldon Larry, your director. Jon Denny and I are in Vancouver scouting locations. Loved your rewrite with the gas station in place of the tollbooth. What do you think of Cheech for the driving instructor? Call us. We're staying at the Ming."

When I was twenty-eight and had written my first teleplay, we had Meryl Streep and a Sheraton Motor Hotel. Now, the better part of a decade later, I'm considering Cheech and dialing a vase.

November 26, 1986: "Hi, Wendy, it's Phylis Geller at the Ming. Ron Silver is interested, but you have to get him a script in New York today. Also, could you bring up some Thanksgiving turkey?"

4 a.m.: "Wen, Ron wants history. He says the character lacks history. I promised him you were working on it."

I can't sleep. I have to flesh out "The Rise and Fall of a Driving Instructor."

November 28, 1986: Waiting at the airport in Vancouver, I indulge my perpetual fear of abandonment. There's no one to meet me. Maybe Streisand replaced Teri and they have all forgotten about me. After most of my fellow passengers have departed, a young man approaches and asks if my name is Wendy. He's sorry, but he thought I was the lady in the mink with the gold Rolex, because she looks like a New York writer. I tell him I must look like a Topeka writer. He doesn't laugh.

Valhalla. The Ming! Actually, it's the Ming Court. And it's neither the motel/vase that I feared nor the grand Canadian Pacific Railway hotel that I secretly hoped for. The Ming is sort of a sweeter version of a Ramada Inn. My room has a glittering view of downtown Vancouver. The city is beautiful—water, hills, skyscrapers. I immediately pass out.

November 29, 1986:   The cast gathers in the basement of the Canadian Broadcasting building for the first reading. Catherine Bach tells me she is doing this small part especially for me. She saw my play *Isn't It Romantic,* and loved it. Furthermore, she has even brought her own furs. I make a note to ask Sheldon if I can build up her role.

The reading goes all right. Teri is from California and doesn't quite understand how anyone could be terrified of turning left. Jon Denny takes me aside. Ron will be arriving tonight, and he expects his history.

I am up until 2 a.m. with a rented typewriter, creating and revising history.

November 30, 1986:   Our first day of shooting and the Ming lobby is rejoicing. Revelers are on hand with streamers and kazoos. However, they are not celebrating our film but Grey Cup weekend, the Canadian Super Bowl, featuring the Hamilton Tiger Cats versus the Edmonton Eskimos.

Sheldon casts Jon Denny and me as walk-ons at the Kaplan School of Driving. I have often heard actors complain that making a movie is boring, that you just sit around. But I am totally fascinated. There is an army here of camera, sound, and lighting people, American and Canadian, to transform three lines of script into a reality.

I watch Teri's face as she reveals anticipation, fear, and a loopy courage. She is no longer a confident actress but a slightly panicked academic. I'm very happy to be back at PBS as a walk-on. At least, I'm happy until Sheldon tells me I've missed my cue and they have to shoot the entire scene again.

A short note on international relations. The series is scheduled to be shown in both Canada and the United States. Before we begin the third take, I notice Jon Denny surreptitiously removing the Canadian flag from a desk. On the fourth take, a Canadian production assistant replaces the Stars and Stripes with a Maple Leaf.

Grey Cup party at the Ming. The Hamilton Tiger Cats blew 'em away.

December 1, 1986: A yellow school bus with a twenty-piece high school marching band arrives on the set. And here's the not-so-subtle difference between plays and movies. In this scene Teri will, by an act of divine intervention, parallel park, pass her test, and be surrounded not only by the marching band, still playing "Little Old Lady from Pasadena," but by all the townspeople at the Motor Vehicle Department as well. Although this isn't precisely cuing the Russian Revolution, trust me, you could never do it Off-Broadway.

December 2, 1986: The parking scene isn't working. There are technical difficulties, and we're already on the twentieth take. I have spent the greater part of the morning huddled near the coffee wagon. Movie crews, like the technical people in the theater, are the best folks to hang out with. Actors want line changes, directors want scene changes, producers will never say exactly what they want; but the crew is a haven, a short-term family.

I am joined by Phylis, our executive producer, and her husband, Fred Pollack, a poet. Fred is calming Phylis about overtime expenditures when suddenly I am ambushed from the rear. Ron taps me on the shoulder with a Xerox of his new scene.

"Wendy, why don't we go over this in my Winnebago?"

Now, a public television Winnebago differs substantially from a Joan Collins Winnebago. Ron and I hover at a fold-down Formica tabletop. OK, he has some points. There are consistency problems. I agree to logic, if Ron agrees not to add his own material. We make a Winnebago pact.

December 3, 1986: It's Hat Day! All members of the crew have arrived in outstanding headgear, including a magenta fortune-teller's turban.

For me Hat Day marks a milestone. When Teri crashes into a police motorcycle, it will be my first stunt ever. The caterer, with whom I've become friends, offers me a congratulatory pickle. He does a beautiful job on a budget.

We wrap—after a few days I'm picking up the lingo—inside a comfortable suburban house. Teri and I pass each other in the hall, and each of us glances at photographs of the five well-groomed children who apparently live here. We share a moment. "Do we envy this life?"

Later, the lady of the house approaches Teri on the

street. She had been an actress in England but gave it up to raise her family. Watching their encounter, the successful actress and the lovely family woman, I decide I want to go home to New York and write. Though my time at the Ming has been inspiring, my colleagues here are working, I am watching.

December 4, 1986: My last day. I give Ron a gift, "A History of Gerry the Driving Instructor, Part I."

"OK, lock it up. Quiet on the set." Peter Dashkewytch, the Canadian first assistant director, seals the room for an intimate scene: Teri, frazzled, alone in her apartment, making a list of her priorities.

But something is not working. Teri feels she is watching her own character. She asks me whether she can borrow the Dartmouth sweatshirt I'm wearing. My couture is making its international debut.

I stop by with Jon to say goodbye to the actors. They are shooting an epilogue for each character. Catherine Bach is wearing a black toga; she appears costumed for Aeschylus. We insist on a group portrait.

Jon Denny walks me to a cab. He is in a great mood. He has reached Candice Bergen at home and persuaded her to be in the next film. Jon tells me that Candice wanted to know whether there was a suite at the Ming.

"And what did you tell her?" I'm back to feeling fond of all that energy.

"I said, 'No suite, but how 'bout a bungalow.' "

March 1987: "Wendy, it's Phylis. We're reshooting a scene and we need your Dartmouth sweatshirt."

I suppose there *are* disadvantages to wearing only originals.

May 1987: "Hey, Wen, this is Jon Denny. I'm with Sheldon at the Ming. We're editing the movie, everyone is very excited. But there's a problem. Ron needs more history."

I reach Jon at the Ming. It's a year later, and I'm a year closer to being cured. *"No,* Jon. Absolutely not."

"Hey, Wen. We're thrilled."

The Good, the Plaid, and the Ugly

A friend of mine from a very good old family recently invited me to spend a summer weekend at her parents' island home in Maine. My friend's parents are retired and now hardly ever make it to "the mainland," let alone down to New York to visit their daughter. As we set out for the weekend, I anticipated a country retreat bathed in chintz, with family photographs taken at lacrosse meets, duck decoys, blueberry-embossed lamp shades, and, at cocktail time, monogrammed Waterford glasses.

I was therefore stunned when, rather than wicker rockers placed kitty-corner to an old English pine table, what I encountered was an acrylic couch covered with a madras bedspread kitty-corner to a plywood-on-cinder-block coffee table. I was invited to sit down, and then we all drank scotch from glasses that came free in a super-size box of Duz. The only part of the weekend that was even vaguely in synch with my fantasy was the still handsome father, who, at age seventy, wearing faded chinos and a red L. L. Bean chamois shirt, pulled out and showed us his plans for the library extension, which he planned to build single-handedly the following summer. He was rugged, with his wire-rimmed glasses and his opinions about Walter Gropius. The entire family, in fact, had opinions about Walter Gropius.

I was impressed. I had a lovely weekend. But frankly, I was also disappointed. That Maine kitchen equipped with Pathmark super-size bottles of diet Coke and J&B was a far cry from the tasteful butler's pantry, recessed lighting, and Pierre Deux curtains I'd been expecting. I kept hoping that the family's conversation would shift from Walter Gropius to how they had coordinated those plaid curtains with their couch. Sadly, my journey to that island helped to confirm a growing suspicion of mine: Only young and aging urban professionals, and Brooklyn and Bronx Brahmin like Woody Allen, Ralph Lauren, and me, like plaid. And we have liked it ever since our Mayflower days. That's the Mayflower Donut Shop, formerly of Fifty-seventh Street in Manhattan.

I will stop right now before I am accused of being anti-urban professional, anti-Brooklyn and anti-Bronx, or, even worse, anti-plaid. Perhaps if I trace my own history and association with plaids, I can justify this sweeping generalization. At which point I will turn my full attention to paisley.

My first encounter with plaid took place more than twenty years ago, during the heyday of Ladybug and Villager shirtwaist dresses. For those who don't remember, they were those delightful cotton A-line numbers with round collars, cinched waists, and a flair at the hips. They were suited to only one kind of figure, yet they were the uniform of millions. On my own sixteen-year-old frame, the chest buttons often pulled a little, the waist snap sometimes popped, and the rounded collar was uniquely unflattering. Most unflattering of all were the versions in blue-gray and magenta madras plaid—they were guaranteed to accentuate the hips *and* to bleed. Just one drop of rain, and there went twenty weeks' allowance.

Looking back, I realize I would have been better off developing an intense early interest in computer science than submitting to the popularity of those madras dresses. But I was determined to train myself to appreciate plaid and the republic for which it stands. I decided that I would curtail my natural preference for bright red and purple in favor of the more subtle joys of blue boxed against beige. I would also train my arm muscles to bulge as if they, and I, preferred squash to pick-up-sticks. Those squash muscles were the only muscles that could do justice to the plaid badge of courage. What I didn't realize back then was that an entire generation of plaid wanna-be's were rigorously training along with me.

My friend Eric was the first man of my acquaintance to wear an L. L. Bean sweater—circa 1970. (It was the blue one with the white specks, or dots.) Eric also deserves credit for introducing me to my first L. L. Bean catalog. By that time I had moved beyond Ladybug shirtwaists, and I had no interest whatsoever in corduroy wrap skirts. Everyone *I* knew wore textured stockings and mini dresses and could have cared less about duck boots. But as I flipped through that catalog, the profusion of plaid flannel shirts and red-and-black goose-hunting jackets made an undeniable impression. And it occurred to me that Eric just might be on to something.

I'm not sure why, a few years later, I was so insecure about assessing styles and forging one of my own. Maybe I was searching for rules that I could eventually break. In any case, I at some point decided that mothers in hats and pumps with daughters in duck boots and bleeding madras dresses must know the secret of life. And that the road to Nirvana must begin with imitating them.

From that moment on, for a while at least, I looked at slipcovers in a new and more appreciative light. Even faded chintz drapes seemed covetable. No home was complete without framed family photographs in its entry-way. Monograms added that special touch, and tiny enamel Battersea boxes imported from England were a daily must. The necessary focus of this total "look" was, of course, plaid. Plaid wing chairs, plaid shades, plaid bedspreads.

I could change my life, my very essence, just by choosing intersecting horizontal and vertical lines. A girl who lived in a studio apartment in Brooklyn could enjoy the same surroundings as a socialite in an eighty-room triplex on Ninety-third and Park. The only difference was the number of rooms at your disposal for filling with plaid.

Frankly, you can fit a lot of Battersea boxes into a studio apartment. My plaid binge ended when I realized that the *last* thing I wanted to be was a socialite in an eighty-room triplex on Ninety-third and Park.

* * *

In recent years, as I've entered midlife, I have developed a great fondness for all things dowdy. I find that I'm most comfortable in faded rooms that resemble dormitory date parlors of the 1930s. I'm perfectly content not to know the decorator, the style, or the fabric. I don't care that the chair I'm putting my feet up on costs $30 rather than $3,000. It can even be plaid, as long as it's also comfortable. Most people would probably think me profoundly unhip in my life-style choices. But I've discovered that I'm happiest when the burden of creating an image is completely off me. Unlike when I was a teenager, I wouldn't even bother making the effort anymore to prove that I like plaid.

What continues to fascinate me, though, is the many others who do. Freeport, Maine, has grown from Mr. Bean's original one-hunting-goods-store village to an outlet megalopolis open for business 24 hours a day, because millions of Americans apparently feel a burning urge to buy plaid at 4 a.m.

But the pinnacle of plaid training is occupied by Ralph Lauren and his emporia. The world I hoped I would encounter on that island in Maine is available for a hefty sum at Ralph's on New Bond Street, London, on Rodeo Drive in Beverly Hills, and at the flagship store on the Upper East Side of Manhattan. My friend Eric's sweater and those corduroy wraparound skirts now have high-priced progeny in cashmere and velvet. Monogrammed glasses, chintz pillows, silver frames for the crew team portraits, and other icons of families with traditional pasts have all been re-created by a visionary from one of New York City's finer boroughs. I have no idea whether Ralph Lauren himself likes plaid, but there's no denying that he sure knew what to do with it.

* * *

I confess that I was secretly delighted the other day when
an invitation to a private white sale turned up in my mailbox. I knew I had arrived, since I was one of the select
two million people who received invitations to this event.
What was even more exciting, though, was that I knew
in advance exactly what I wanted to buy. My hopes were
set on an ensemble of those pink-and-white oxford cloth
sheets and a new pair of plaid pillowcases—just for old
time's sake and as a memento of my Down East Brooklyn
Yankee roots.

To Live and Diet

Weight is the bane of my existence. When I riseth up and when I falleth down. It is a shadow that always follows me. Even when we separate for a time, we are never really parted. As I ramble through life, whatever be my goal, I will unfortunately always keep my eye upon the doughnut and not upon the whole.

I first decided that I had a weight problem during free swim at Camp Navajo in Honesdale, Pennsylvania. Among eight-year-olds of that time, the measure of a lithe and perfectly silhouetted body was taken by standing with both legs together and creating three perfect "diamonds"—between the ankles, knees, and upper thighs.

There was hardly a breeze, never mind a diamond, between my early thighs. That summer I vowed that when I turned ten, the age of complexity, I would go on a diet. Double-digit ages augured boys, and boys meant I better get myself a diamond.

As I look back now, the irony is that I was not particularly overweight at the time and that the girls with the three apertures looked their best on a horse. At Camp Navajo there were clearly two factions: those who took a bite of a cupcake and lost interest and those who devoured the cake only to ravage the paper. At age eight I joined the ranks of the savage cupcakivores. And once I determined that I was a woman of substance, I never again willfully opted for a sleeveless T-shirt.

I saw my first diet doctor when I was a sophomore in high school. Oddly enough, I was not particularly overweight at that time, either. But those of us who came of age with Jean Shrimpton and Twiggy were given to understand that what was most desirable was having not just three diamonds between our ankles, knees, and thighs, but a single gaping canyon.

My high school diet doctor had a drawer full of pills: pink, red, blue. Each week there was a new selection for breakfast, lunch, and dinner that he would dole out as he sat behind his desk polishing off a bagel with lox and cream cheese. I have no idea what was in those pills, but I do remember a history class during which I could scarcely contain my enthusiasm for the causes of the Franco-Prussian War. Bismarck flipped out when he received the "Ems dispatch" from King William, thereby starting the war: Or maybe Bismarck falsified the telegram in order to make the Germans think the French

ambassador had insulted the Prussian king. I remember
my weight more than I remember the details. On July 19,
1870, France declared war on Prussia, and in my junior
year I weighed 130 pounds. It was a heady time.

A hallmark of women's higher education in the early seventies was an institution called, at least at my college,
Milk and Crackers. The arrival of 10 p.m. was marked
daily with a light snack of graham crackers, peanut butter, and Marshmallow Fluff. (This, it perhaps goes without saying, was in the pre–salad bar days.)

At college I developed Wendy's Hibernation Nutrition
Plan. Milk and Crackers for the New England winter,
blue and red pills over the New York summer. Some of
my forward-looking friends experimented with anorexia;
the true groundbreakers dabbled in bulimia. My own
doctor-sanctioned summer shedding inevitably brought
such annual back-to-school comments as "Guess who
lost weight" or "You look completely different. I didn't
recognize you." Funny, I always recognized them.

I realized then that my weight, the kilos of my
body, was not a private matter but a topic for public
consideration.

My least favorite diet doctor (and since the bagel-munch-
ing pill dispenser I've had many) was a hypnotist whom
a manicurist recommended to my mother. Apparently the
manicurist's niece had dropped two hundred pounds because of this doctor. I was in graduate school when it
was gently suggested that I take the train from New
Haven into the city for a consultation with this distinguished specialist.

In the hypnotist's office I breathed in and out three times while a voice—it sounded to me like a cross between Tom Carvel's and the Crazy Eddie man's—told me to relax and imagine the joys of fresh fruit, vegetables, and broiled fish, no butter. We taped our sessions, and I was instructed to play the tape whenever I thought about Fluff. On the train home, while my fellow commuters were listening to Aretha through their earphones, I was being brainwashed with r-e-s-p-e-c-t for melons, honeydews, please no pears.

Ever since I left school and began an independent adult life, it seems that every three years or so I decide to take myself in hand. Generally this spring cleaning, this pulling myself together, coincides with an important birthday or, more likely, a new romance. In total, I have shed at least one hundred pounds for various boyfriends. Most of the boyfriends, however, have preferred me lumpy. In fact, the love of my life to date was at his most passionate on an enchanted evening when my hair was unwashed and I registered on my Terraillon scale a record weight that I have yet to pass. But, still, somewhere in me is the belief that losing forty pounds would herald a clean slate, a new beginning, a chance for redemption. The physical would lead the spiritual. In other words, liking myself means liking diet Jell-O.

In these spurts of self-control, self-discipline, and self-reliance, I have encountered serious, even successful, diet and behavior modification plans. Actually, some of my most productive periods have coincided with the times when I was busy keeping track of my Wasa Crispbread intake for Maggie, my Diet Center buddy. I find photographs of "before and after" achievers—Weight

Watchers valedictorians—far more impressive than any pin-up of Heather Locklear or Princess Stephanie. A few years ago, at an obesity group, I met a nice, rather substantial man who told me that women refused to sit next to him on buses. Later he wrote me a note saying that he had lost weight and that he hoped I was well and happy. I still think about that man occasionally. I think about how he could move to London, Paris, Los Angeles—someplace where no one would know his past—and start again. He could be someone else, with the bus seats beside him always occupied. Except . . .

Except it's always there. If tomorrow, through the miracle of liposuction, I weighed ninety pounds, I still would never dream of wearing the Sonia Rykiel dress, the one in the Madison Avenue window that is the width of a fabric bolt. That dress is for the other faction. I could never go to Le Cirque, eat a fig, play with dessert, and complain that I ate too much. Only thin people do that. And I could never feel completely at home among the girls in leather pants and spike heels or strapless cocktail dresses. We parted company at age eight. No matter what happens, we are different. I've been a player for the other side. I can't abandon the home team. When the girls in the strapless cocktail dresses say they are enormous, I smile or change the subject. Size is relative.

When I embark on any new romantic or career venture, there is for me always the same bottom line. Namely, I will assume that, no matter what happens, no matter how deeply I fall in love or how successful the project, if anything goes wrong it is because I prefer buttered rolls to bran flakes for breakfast. That is, the stock market almost crashed because I refuse to do aerobics. Or: I don't have fear of intimacy, my date has fear-o-flesh. OK, maybe I'm exaggerating a little. But the paranoia, the impulse to blame everything on excess tonnage, is undeniably real.

More than anything, even more than a secret desire never to be asked by the saleslady behind the stocking counter at Bonwit's whether I shouldn't really be buying the queen-size pantyhose, is my hope, my fantasy, that someday this horribleness will all go away. Yes, triglycerides are bad, cholesterol is bad, heart problems are bad, and lack of muscle tone on someone so young is horrendous. But so is such a superficial standard for rating human quality. We treat melons with more dignity. At least we wait to make a judgment until we know what's inside.

A diet counselor once told me that all overweight people are angry with their mothers and channel their frustrations into overeating. So I guess that means all thin people are happy, calm, and have resolved their Oedipal entanglements. It is, I'm afraid, universally accepted now that an overweight woman is somehow an unfulfilled, unhappy woman. Oprah Winfrey may have made millions of dollars and surpassed Phil Donahue in the ratings, but she had a double chin. Not until she lived on liquid protein, lost sixty pounds, and started looking like everybody else did she find—or so we are told—true happiness.

I wish I had the legs of every girl pictured leaping in those designer-fashion magazine ads. But I don't. And even if I lived on Wasa Crispbread alone, I probably never would. What I'm waiting for is the day when I, and even the three-diamonders, just won't care. Or better yet, when no one will even notice.

High
Adventure
in the
Balkans

I still think about Rumania all the time. Waiting in line to cast my vote for president at a public school at York Avenue and Seventy-seventh Street, I wonder about the next Election Day in Timişoara. At a friend's wedding I watch Aspen-tanned bodies swathed in Bulgari jewels boogaloo to "Hot Hot Hot," and I flash on a Rumanian synagogue with its doors and windows bricked shut. In a newspaper detailing the Ceausescus' illicit hoarding of goods in the name of the Rumanian people I find a minor item noting that all typewriters in Rumania had to be registered. And immediately I return to the summer of 1988—a year before the Berlin Wall came down, a year before the Prague Autumn, a year before the Ceausescus' trial and execution —and that incident on the Vršac/Vatin border.

* * *

My only previous trip to Eastern Europe had been in 1967, when I served as a *Herald Tribune* World Youth Forum delegate to Yugoslavia. That summer, before my fellow delegates and I entered Wharton, Yale, Colgate, or Mount Holyoke College, we set out to expand our views and challenge our perspectives. We made the most of our visit behind the Iron Curtain. Some of the more adventurous of us even managed to track down the writer Milovan Djilas, who had been imprisoned after the publication of his *Conversations with Stalin* in 1962. We visited Djilas in his apartment, and our conversation there was unforgettable: "Mr. Djilas, we American youths want to know—what was Stalin really like?" Djilas paid us the supreme compliment of taking us seriously.

In my heart I am a perpetual World Youth Forumer. I still want to expand my viewpoint, challenge my perspective, and search for the Djilas apartment. I know a quick transatlantic shopping trip to Harrods can be a lift, but sometimes what a girl really needs is to be shaken up a bit.

In June 1988, I acted as chaperon for my niece Pamela Wasserstein at the 2nd World Youth and Peace Chess Festival in Timişoara, Rumania. Pamela was a contender in the Age-Ten-and-Under category.

We had everything perfectly planned. My sister Sandra would escort Pamela on the first leg of her journey. Next, I would wing in and spend a week with our prodigy. Finally, my sister-in-law Chris, Pamela's mother, would appear for the last rounds of the championship. In retrospect, I can think of better places to run family relay races than Timişoara.

Any of you who might be planning to escort your niece to a future chess championship should be advised that the preferred New York–Timişoara route involves a flight to Belgrade, followed by what is called a two-hour drive. But not to worry—almost everyone in the Belgrade airport speaks English.

When I arrive in Belgrade, I head immediately for the predetermined location where I am to meet the car and driver reserved for me in advance by my travel agent. An accommodating man behind the Avis counter hands me a note left by my sister Sandra:

> The ride to Timişoara is a piece of cake. Pamela expects you around suppertime, and if she's not in her hotel suite she'll be in the dining room with the American chess team. Also, stop in a store in Yugoslavia and get Pamela Coke, fruit, and chocolates.

My driver, Bob Slobodan, greets me cordially and explains that his name means Bob Freeman. I'm not sure whether Bob is a Serbian landsman or a Croatian libertarian, but he is definitely on our side. He drives a black Mercedes and wears his clinging blue shirt open to a very Continental latitude.

"I like English," Bob says, offering me a cigarette and smiling into the rearview mirror. "I've been to Germany, Italy, Spain, France. But I like English. English is very good." Bob's a regular Adriatic Belmondo.

The Yugoslavian countryside was beautiful in 1967, and it remains beautiful. Teal-blue tiled church roofs glisten in the sunlight. Bob and I stop at a village grocery store to load up for my niece. I buy Coke, chocolate, coffee, Gruyère, and crackers in quantities that recall the care packages of salami and Twizzlers licorice that sympathetic parents delivered to my summer camp when I was a child. This particular care package costs less than $10 in dinars. Bob tells me that this amount is more than he makes in a month.

As we drive through yet another village, my thoughts drift to Miss Caris Hall, my favorite high school history teacher, who explained to us Advanced Placement girls how the assassination of Archduke Ferdinand in Sarajevo was the opening salvo of World War I. Twenty years after the explanation, and nearly three-quarters of a century after the event itself, here in all unlikelihood *I* am, riding through the Yugoslavian countryside like a sort of show-biz Mary Poppins, the designated escort of an international chess champion.

"Here is very, very good," Bob assures me. "Yugoslavia is very, very good. Rumania is bad. There is nothing in Rumania. Rumania is very, very bad."

The backup on the Vršac/Vatin border makes Friday-night traffic on the Long Island Expressway seem a breeze. Bob brings our Mercedes to a halt and walks past the fifteen cars in front of us, directly up to the head customs officer. I watch his arms fly up and down as he negotiates for our speedy departure. He returns to the car muttering and smoking.

"You see those people over there?" Bob says, pointing to a family picnicking by the curb. "They are poor people. They go to shop in Rumania. Rumania is cheap. But there's nothing in Rumania."

After at least two hours pass, it's time for our side to

make a move. Bob offers his passport and mine to the Yugoslavian border guard and mutters something about my American citizenship. The guard looks at me, looks at Bob, and we are out of there quicker than you can say Slobodan. Piece of cake.

And that's when the problem of the goddamn puddle arises. Like most puddles, this one owes its existence, one assumes, to a thundershower, an unexpected dip in the road, or both. Bob, like most drivers faced with such a puddle, decides to circumvent it. It's this decision that brings me into my first contact with the Rumanian police.

On the Vršac/Vatin border can you trust your car to the man who wears the star? A young guard with a poised rifle approaches us, and I quickly understand that in Rumania you don't decide all by yourself to circumvent a puddle. In Rumania even a black Mercedes—or especially a black Mercedes—must remain in its lane, puddle or no puddle.

Bob is pissed. I'm tired. It's past nine o'clock, and my niece is certainly no longer in the dining room with the American chess team. I imagine hysterical transatlantic phone calls between Timişoara and New York: I'm an irresponsible aunt and an eccentric unmarried daughter. Only a Bachelor Girl would end up stranded on the Rumanian border without access to a telephone. This whole unpleasant scenario is a far cry from *Mary Poppins*.

When an officer in a bright blue uniform emerges from a hutlike office, the drivers and passengers from the vehicles all around us immediately drop their picnics and open their car hoods, trunks, and doors. But the officer walks directly toward us. Bob smiles, hands our passports over, shrugs, and once again says something about my being American. This time he also mentions the chess tournament. Bob believes that because I am an

American citizen and because I am riding in a Mercedes, this is going to be easy. What he doesn't realize is that his passenger, a former World Youth Forumer, understands that she represents America. And, as an American, she must tell the truth, the whole truth, and nothing but the truth.

"Your name is Vasserstein?"

I smile. "Yes."

"You speak another language, Vasserstein?"

"No. Well, a little French."

"Vat do you do, Vasserstein?"

I look at his face and realize that this officer is only about nineteen years old. I can't tell whether he's repeating my name because it sounds suspiciously German to him or because he thinks I'm a distant relative of Frankenstein. "I'm going to a chess tournament. My niece, little girl, is chess champion."

"Vasserstein, vat vork do you do?"

If I were smart, if I were less parochial, if all those pamphlets that arrive at my house from PEN, Helsinki Watch, Amnesty International had even made a dent, I would say that I am a housewife and a mother. But those tales of repression, censorship, the abolishment of artistic and human rights couldn't possibly have anything to do with me. I'm represented by International Creative Management.

"I am a writer. I write plays. *Une écrivain pour le théâtre. Dramatiste.*"

"Vasserstein, are you married?" For the first time since this dialogue began, Bob looks back at me. I feel like I'm on "Wheel of Fortune" and Bob knows all the missing letters and I don't.

"No. I'm not married."

When he hears my marital status, the guard immediately turns around and walks away. My mother is right. It's a global humiliation.

Bob sits down on our luggage in despair.

"What's wrong, Bob?" Are they going to keep me out of the country because I'm single? How many available men are there in Rumania? Is the ratio that bad? It's terrible in New York, too, but we still let some single women in over the bridge from New Jersey.

"Rumania is terrible! Terrible!" Bob is fed up with the guard and with me. If he had known I was a playwright and single, he would never have taken this job. Western women are so naive. They think just because they can lunch at the Century Association, the whole world will open up for them. Bob wishes that I were Sam Shepard or David Mamet.

My interrogator returns from the station house with a higher-up. I know he is a superior because his star is bigger and brighter. He is also slightly more refined, slightly more handsome—Kevin Kline without the smile, without the mustache.

"Hey, Joy! Joy!" he announces. I look around. "Joy, that is the name on your passport." For a moment I have forgotten that my middle name is Joy, and my interrogator is deriving some pleasure from this. Seeing his smile, I am transported to another time, another Europe. A Europe that I don't know but that my parents and their generation will never forget. "Joy, why do you have a fifteen-day visa when you say you come for five days?"

"I'm going to the chess championship in Timişoara." I don't know why I have a fifteen-day visa. Ask Elaine at VTS Travel.

Kevin Kline is waiting for me to explain further. Finally he says, "You speak another language?"

"No. Not really."

"Open your suitcase."

Out on the Vršac/Vatin border come my Belle France dresses, my Chanel skin program, and my Christian Dior lace-top panties. Kevin opens up all my makeup bags.

Kevin, let me explain. I use Aqua-fresh because I like the mint. I wear Guerlain perfume, L'Heure Bleue, and Parure, which, by the way, you can't get in the States, even at Bergdorf's. And I don't wear much makeup, but I'm in the process of teaching myself how to use base.

I believe he's finished. I believe I can put Bob out of his misery, and we can be on our way. But then Kevin pulls the book I am currently reading from the side pocket of my suitcase. He shows the book—*A Life* by Elia Kazan—to the first interrogator. "He is Rumanian. This is a political book!" The two of them nod. And for a moment all three of them—Kevin, the nineteen-year-old, and the book-jacket photograph of Kazan—stare at me expectantly.

Goddamn it! Someone in the Belgrade airport, an informer or the secret police, must have recognized me as the Youth Forum girl who visited Milovan Djilas's apartment back in the summer of 1967. Djilas was punished for Stalin; I will be similarly punished for Kazan.

"Il est un directeur. La cinéma. A Streetcar Named Desire. La Mort d'un Salesman."

Kevin is flipping through the book. The nineteen-year-old interrogator joins him. They glide past the chapters on Marlon Brando, Tennessee Williams, Marilyn Monroe, and Harold Clurman. The episode with HUAC is fast approaching.

I imagine Elia Kazan being interviewed on "Today," "Good Morning, America," and all the evening news programs: "You can't blame *me* for her incarceration."

"He is Rumanian, no?" Kevin continues to stare at the book's cover while the nineteen-year-old roams further into my suitcase. Who knows what other subversive works, like *People* and *Time,* are in there?

"Vat is this?" The interrogator has found two manuscript copies of *The Heidi Chronicles,* the play I'm currently working on.

"It's my play."

"Vat is it, Vasserstein?"

Well, it's a comedy. A social history. It's about an art historian named Heidi who grew up in Chicago and went to Vassar. It's about two of Heidi's male friends—one of whom becomes a gay pediatrician, the other a Jewish journalist. Are there gay pediatricians and Jewish journalists in Rumania?

They begin to read through the script.

Kevin, do you think I have second-act problems? How about the restaurant scene? Should I keep it in? What do *you* think of the ending?

"This is yours?" Their dark eyes peer at me.

"Yes, this is mine. I am a *dramatiste.*"

Kevin and the nineteen-year-old look at each other. They turn away from me and retreat into the station house.

"Bob, Bob, what's going on here?" I'm more than a little anxious.

"Rumania!" Bob smokes and shakes his head. "Rumania!" he mutters.

The guards remain in the station house for at least another hour. I feel guilty about holding up all the cars around us. They are stripped and ready for action, while our hosts are inside reading *The Heidi Chronicles.* Maybe they've put in a call to Robert Brustein: Bob, Wendy was at the Yale School of Drama when you were dean; what did you think of her plays? Give our regards to Andrei Serban and Liviu Ciulei.

Finally they emerge. *The Heidi Chronicles* is not a plot to overthrow Nicolae Ceauşescu. We are free to go.

Bob careers away from the border into the Rumanian night.

There are no streetlights on the highway. The trunks of trees along the road are painted white, and car headlights shine on them. Before we reach our destination, we are twice forced to stop at police roadblocks. I believe the word is out. Ask her for the book and read the Marilyn Monroe section.

We reach the hotel at midnight. I give Bob thousands of dinars (which probably don't amount to much) as a tip and proceed directly up to my niece's room. I can't bear even to check in to my own room. I couldn't stand being asked yet one more question.

Pamela is alone in her room reading *Frankenstein*. She tells me there's no food in Rumania, just fried cheese, tasteless tomatoes, and mystery meat. So we decide to have a midnight picnic with my Yugoslavian booty.

Long into the morning, in that hotel room with lace curtains and dark, velvet-covered furniture, I recount to my chess-champion niece my adventures on the Vršac/ Vatin border. Pamela picks up my copy of Elia Kazan's *A Life* and looks at the jacket photograph. "Aunt Wendy, were you going to start a revolution with this man?"

During the time I spent in Timişoara, I committed not a single word to paper. I write in order to express myself, my thoughts, my individual voice—and in Rumania such an act of self-expression, like the decision made on one's own to circumvent a puddle, was for decades not only suspect but unacceptable. My respect for the artists who lived under such a repressive regime and who nonetheless maintained the strength and courage to continue their work is beyond admiration, closer to awe.

I'll never forget those policemen leafing through the manuscript of my play. On the night when I saw the lights for *The Heidi Chronicles* come up on Broadway, my thoughts involuntarily returned to the border of the Socialist Republic of Rumania. I am not a Mary Poppins. I am not an eccentric wandering aunt. What I am is a very lucky girl.

The New Capitalist Tool

On a recent summer afternoon a few actress friends of mine gathered in my apartment for a reunion. We ordered in chicken tarragon and shortbread cookies from E.A.T. Those with children passed around the requisite photographs of their offspring. We gossiped, intimacies were renewed, and soon we were confessing to one another our disconcerting cholesterol levels and our deepest, darkest biopsy scares.

Eventually, as afternoon moved into evening, we hooked up the VCR for a private screening of the movie version of Clare Boothe Luce's *The Women*. After all the medical true confessions signaling the onset of middle age that had dominated the afternoon, it was definitely time to change topics. Moreover, this gathering was taking place at the instigation of our mutual friend Anne Cattaneo, the literary manager of The Lincoln Center Theater, who at the time was considering a revival or updated version of Mrs. Luce's play. My actress friends and I were to serve as Anne's panel of qualified experts on the project's viability.

The giggles began with the credits. There was Norma Shearer's mother depicted literally as a wise old owl, and the scheming Joan Crawford as a leopard, a beautiful clawing cat.

"I want the hat! I want the hat!" we squealed when Rosalind Russell and her chapeau appeared.

For those who don't remember the story line: Perfect Norma Shearer, the delightful, beautiful, gracious, kind, and good Westchester matron Mary Haines, is informed by her bitchy, up-to-no-good, pretending-to-care-about-her-women-friends friend that her husband, the good, kind, very rich, very handsome Stephen Haines, is having an affair with Crystal, a low, scheming, no-good, sexed-up, conniving, and ambitious dame who works behind the perfume counter at Saks Fifth Avenue.

Since Mary Haines's pride is wounded, she confronts Stephen, refuses to take him back, and soon finds herself in a car filled with other "first wives" on the train to Reno. What Mary learns by the end of the saga is to screw her pride and to go out there and fight like a feline to get her Stephen back. A claw for a claw is the law of the jungle.

"Period piece! Period piece!" my guests howled at the TV screen by midway into the film.

"You'll get killed if you try to update something like this," was offered as a subtle piece of advice to Anne.

"Yeah, do it only for the hats," was the final consensus.

"Thank God so much has changed," the Norma Shearer of our group sighed.

Frankly, I agreed. That is, I agreed until I came across the August 29, 1989, issue of *Fortune* magazine. The cover story of this particular issue was "The CEO's Second Wife: How She Changes the Man and the Manager." Thirty years after Mrs. Luce's cautionary tale, dress designer Carolyne Roehm, looking lovely in green brocade and I-have-no-idea-how-precious-the-stone earrings, graced the cover of *Fortune* with the byline "Carolyne Roehm, whose husband is Henry Kravis." It was only the second time in the history of *Fortune* that a woman made a solo appearance on the cover of the magazine. And she got there, it seems, not by racking up corporate accomplishments (which, in fact, Ms. Roehm has) but by exercising all the feminine skills of a "Crystal" with class.

The second wives celebrated in this *Fortune* article are a new breed. Or, rather, they are living proof that the fundamental things do apply as time goes by. These women are certainly not the "superwomen" of the seventies and eighties we have all heard so much about. The "superwoman" attempted to "have it all," and by now it's common knowledge that being "omni-perfect" can cause wrinkles in a marriage and a career as well as the complexion. Besides, what these second wives seem to have figured out is that it's obviously much easier to "have it all" if a zillionaire is paying for it. Smart girls can be so dumb!

Rather than "superwomen," these second wives are what I'd like to call "superfelines." When an available CEO comes on the market, they are out there scratching for him. And the supreme triumph, it seems—the ticket to the cover of *Fortune*—is not only snagging your man but keeping him. In other words, one significant way in which the world has changed in the decades since *The Women* is that nowadays poor sweet dopey Mary Haines wouldn't stand a chance in hell.

A "superwoman" needed to score an A in every subject. A "superfeline" must get an A+ in husbandry. And if an A− in a design or cosmetics career enables her to maintain that A+, then a thriving, glamorous but unthreatening career is allowed the second wife. These are, after all, trophy wives.

According to *Fortune*, "the way that a second marriage differs most dramatically from the first can be summed up in a single word, 'children.' There usually aren't any." Marriage and child rearing—the two-part cornerstone of the fifties nuclear family, as well as the focus of the earnest have-it-all seventies—are at cross-purposes for these "superfelines" of the nineties. If a woman is going to be the CEO's dream home-entertainment unit, the precious reward of his later life, then he certainly doesn't want her squandering her valuable playtime at a party for actual six-year-olds.

What's most startling to me about this *Fortune* article is that its essential purpose is not to acknowledge these second wives as individuals but, rather, to applaud them for "how they change the man and the manager." Apparently when America's CEOs spend their out-of-office hours being properly entertained at discreet dinner parties and gala premieres at the opera, they become energized and easier to work with. Corporate America therefore depends on forty well-groomed women who maintain twenty-three-inch waistlines and up-to-the-minute invitation lists. Thank heaven for little girls.

* * *

Looking back, it seems the ladies at my reunion and I were hopelessly misinformed. The goals of well-bred American women have not changed so radically. In fact, much like Rosalind Russell's hat, certain familiar, decades-old goals seem to be very much back in vogue. But then again the term "well bred" might be somewhat misleading here since, according to *Fortune,* the histories and backgrounds of these celebrated second wives tend to be mysterious. As in the case of Crystal, these women's greatest inventions may just be themselves.

During my freshman year of college a debutante I knew would read aloud the Sunday *New York Times* wedding announcements in the common room of our dormitory and openly pronounce, "She did well" or "She did lousy." As the winds of feminism later blew into that fading chintz lounge, I remember feeling ecstatic because it seemed that the days of that "did well" list were numbered at last. But apparently the typical CEO's need for feminine wiles are more durable than a passing social current.

The quality of life for the second wife, beyond retaining the man and the manager, is never discussed in *Fortune* magazine. Are these second wives finding fulfillment in their mega-marriages? How stressful is the looming terror of the third wife ("How She Nurses the Man and the Manager")? The happiness of these women is assumed to be synonymous with doing well financially. Even the characters on "Dynasty" know better than that. We haven't come such a long way, baby, if the ultimate privilege for women is in being a first-class support system.

Pappagallo Jungle

A friend of mine was considering sending his four-year-old daughter to a cram course for the nursery school equivalent of the Scholastic Aptitude Test. He said he couldn't imagine what his daughter's future would be if she wasn't accepted into the school of his choice. When my friend asked my advice, I found myself admitting a truth I had never before come out with publicly. I was a Dalton School reject.

I remember the humiliation as if it were yesterday and, of course, I also remember that it wasn't entirely the school's fault. If I had to take an entrance exam for the Dalton School today, there's still a good chance I would be doomed.

It happened in the spring of 1963. My family was

planning to move from Brooklyn to Manhattan, and so we entered, unassuming, into the fast and fabulous world of the New York City private school system. Before the move, I was a student at the Brooklyn Ethical Culture School. There I played Portia in the eighth-grade production of *Julius Caesar* and was particularly advanced at dancing to the colors in Prospect Park. Our dance instructor, Mrs. Janovsky, would beat a tambourine as she rhythmically called out, "Red," "Yellow," "Purple," and we students would in turn express our most visceral connection to each color. It wasn't Summerhill, but it wasn't Bronx Science either.

The world of New York City private schools—Brearley, Spence, Dalton, et al.—was completely foreign to me. In fact, I thought that to have a school named after you, you had to be a president, an inventor, or have the initials P.S. Of course I also didn't know that Manhattan went so far north of Fifty-seventh Street. And I didn't realize that beyond the theater district and Macy's there was a whole residential life going on. To a born-and-bred Brooklynite, "the city" was a place where you went to shop or to take in a show, and then you went home. You certainly didn't spend the night or take a test there in the morning.

I basically believe that most of my family's impressions about schools came from my brother's opinions of the girls he met at high school dances. There was someone from Dalton who had blond, straight hair parted on the side, a mid-sixties Dorothy Lamour. And there was a young lady from Brearley who was obsessed with *The Great Gatsby*. Both of these recommendations led my mother to make inquiries.

Brearley, at the time, seemed more concerned that I hadn't studied French in elementary school than impressed with my Portia or my yellow interpretations. As I recall, my mother and I were both intimidated. We never arranged to take a tour of the school or scheduled an interview. And, in fact, my brother never actually dated the girl who was obsessed with *Gatsby*.

We did, however, pay a visit to Dalton, which in 1963 was still an all-women's school. I remember peeking into the assembly hall and counting row after row of heads with meticulously parted hair and row after row of feet with Pappagallo shoes. Surely if I went to school there I would also be able to wear those pink, paper-thin slippers in the snow.

I've never been a big fan of standardized testing. I've always felt encouraged by the story of the boy who filled out his S.A.T. answer sheet in the shape of a Christmas tree and scored a 763. Mostly what I remember of my Dalton entrance test is the blank piece of paper on which we were supposed to "be creative." Since my drawing skills were (and still are) easily outstripped by the average four-year-old, I decided to combine my literary and artistic abilities. I drew a tree and quoted Joyce Kilmer's immortal "I think that I shall never see / A poem lovely as . . ." a you know what.

As I was drawing, I looked around the room at the girls with discreet bands of silver on their fingers and decided that they all belonged to a world I wasn't part of. Though their feet were pink and preppy, they were unmistakably worldly and "artistic." Their days were no doubt filled with high-minded pastimes. They would never dance to the colors.

My family, however, became determined that I should go to Dalton. After all, I'd receive a proper education, I'd move beyond Joyce Kilmer, my brother would get invited to more high school dances and meet more girls with straight hair parted on the side, and we would quickly assimilate into Upper East Side Manhattan.

On the day of my interview at Dalton, my mother turned out in an uncharacteristically conservative suit, urgently tasteful, and I wore a turquoise mohair coat that today someone in some thrift shop on Avenue A would find divinely retro.

"So, what are your interests, dear?" An older woman in a Marimekko dress was trying to get to know me as a person.

"Well, history, theater," I answered.

"Our girls pursue many of their own interests." She went on to tell me about a girl who traveled to Egypt and was so excited by her trip that she wrote a book about it her sophomore year.

This is where the turning point came. I was twelve at the time, and I knew I could say that I wanted to choreograph my own play, write a book, pursue my own interests, but I didn't feel like it. I didn't want to be one of this woman's girls. It was that simple.

"Why do you want to come to Dalton, dear?" She was working the room. Trying to get a conversation going.

I surreptitiously put a piece of gum in my mouth and began chewing.

My mother turned to me. "Honey, tell her why you want to go to Dalton."

"I don't," I blurted out with the thickest Brooklyn accent imaginable. The Lords of Flatbush had nothing on me. I continued chewing and even burst a tiny bubble. "Look, lady, I want to go to public school with my friends."

Now I might have been a Dalton reject even if I hadn't delivered that statement. The Joyce Kilmer sketch alone probably would have been sufficient cause for exclusion. But my mother will never forget that moment. Her hope for me, her great expectations, went soaring out the window.

Shortly afterward I began behaving myself at school interviews. And I was accepted at the Calhoun School, which was also an all-women's school at the time. The girls there wore Pappagallos, too. But Calhoun did not have the cachet of Dalton. I remember how the mother of my high school boyfriend (he was very smart and went to Horace Mann) was always slightly miffed at his choice of lady friend. After all, both of his sisters attended Dalton.

It's twenty-five years now since my high school interviews. And the world and I have both completely evolved. I know this because I recently had an opportunity to spend an evening with the headmistress of Brearley.

When, at dinner, the headmistress of Brearley asked me where I went to high school, I immediately responded that I had graduated from Mount Holyoke. When she asked again, I covered my mouth and whispered, "Calhoun."

The truth is, I really wanted to put a stick of gum in my mouth and belt, "Look, lady, for your information, I was a Dalton reject." But instead I was well behaved. In part, I suppose, because there might come a day when I'll be dragging my own daughter to an interview at Brearley. Here's hoping she won't take after her mother.

The
Razor's
Edge

emember body hair? In 1970 I took part in a consciousness-raising group in western Massachusetts at which a doctoral candidate in English simplified all political stances with one sweeping agenda. According to her, "Body hair is the last frontier." The good guys—or should I say the good persons?—fell on the furry side. The doctoral candidate's credo was quite simple: "Either you shave your legs or you don't." And if you did shave, you were beyond unliberated. You were seriously Peck & Peck.

My first confrontation with body hair (specifically, the leg variety) occurred on the night before my eighth-grade graduation. Throughout the preceding year, as my friends Nancy, Susan, Sherry, and Starr had each emerged suddenly shapelier and devoid of stubble, my mother had repeatedly warned me about becoming "a slave to your legs." I couldn't understand why my class-mates' mothers were evidently advising them to choose physical attractiveness over emancipation. Of course, it's possible that their mothers stayed out of it and that my friends were becoming chained to their calves of their own free will. Eighth grade is often a turning point in self-determination.

For the commencement ceremony I carefully selected a tummy-lift panty girdle (this was before Madison Ave-nue coined the euphemism "control-top"), sunkist hose, and white pumps with a low heel (to show that I, like Jacqueline Kennedy, was a lady) and an impossibly pointy toe (to demonstrate that in my own way I could compete with any Dawn, Debbie, or Donna on "American Bandstand"). I left the mowing issue open to last-minute debate.

My mother's warning had so alarmed me that I be-lieved just one graze, one tiny trim, and the following week an entire Maine timberland forest would be flour-ishing below my knees. So I decided to consult an expert. I dialed my best friend, Susan—who, incidentally, was the kind of girl who not only knew about legs but was also well versed in eye shadow and blush. That evening, after three hours of telecommunal deliberations, my mother had the audacity to pick up the receiver and ask me to hang up. This intrusion so angered me that I made a grand gesture. I shaved my legs.

The next day I appeared at my eighth-grade gradua-tion wearing white pointy pumps, pantyhose, and at least eight Band-Aids on each leg. Midway I had run out of the sheer strips and, in desperation, had borrowed my brother's more decorative Stars and Stripes adhesives. My classmate Anthony Giuffrida expressed his condolences for my getting the measles at graduation. Clearly I hadn't achieved the effect I'd been hoping for.

There are many women with histories of nicks and woes who come to a crossroad when they discover waxing. I first encountered waxing at college. A woman who lived on the same dormitory floor as I did, and who had replaced all her standard dorm furniture with white wicker, asked me if I would hold her while she waxed her legs. I had no clue as to what she expected of me; I honestly had no idea what she was even talking about. When I consented, she began a process that reminded me of a public television program on the Pilgrims making beeswax candles. I was flabbergasted. This girl was not only a slave to her legs, she was involved in a kinky sadomasochistic relationship with them. Surely no date with any Amherst boy could be worth that agony. Furthermore, I was certain that no boy would ever turn his legs into a human wick for *her*. (The wax woman, I feel compelled to add, became the first girl on our floor to get engaged.)

Frankly, I have always found body hair a hassle. I greatly admire those women in locker rooms who walk into the shower with a beach pail containing cellulite foam, cellulite mitts, shaving cream, Lady Someone razors, Krizia body lotion, and Nina Ricci *eau de toilette*. They inevitably emerge wrapped in a simple towel, perfumed, smoothed, defurred, and perfect. I wonder whether these women actually enjoy the ritual or whether it is simply part of their daily lives, like saying hello when they answer the phone. Maybe my mother made a mistake in advising me that body hair was optional. Maybe I'd be emerging perfumed and poised if only she'd told me that its removal was essential and directly responsible for self-fulfillment and meaningful relationships.

A few years ago when *Time* and *Newsweek* both announced that short skirts were making a comeback, I couldn't help wondering what a certain Massachusetts doctoral candidate's position on those hemlines would be. Most likely she's remained no-nonsense, buys sensible Weejuns from Bass, and has no opinions on the matter of skirt lengths. But it is also possible that she could make quite a healthy case for dark brown L'eggs, the kind that make calves look trimmer and depilatory work irrelevant. Or she could adopt an even bolder stance and declare that body hair is no longer the last frontier. Maybe we've conquered it and moved on. Westward Hosiery!

Recently I attended a dinner party where a dentist who sat next to me outlined at great length the plans for her imminent wedding. She told me how ecstatic she was about almost everything; the glaring exception was that her current Saturday ritual might have to be sacrificed. It seems that every Saturday morning the dentist made her way to Georgette Klinger's beauty salon, slipped into a white robe, and joined Miss Michelle in a discreet sound-proof booth for a leg or occasional bikini wax. (I have nothing to say about bikini waxes except thank heaven no one's ever asked me to hold her while she had one.) The dentist admitted that it was a slight extravagance, but she said she worked very hard all week and this was her pain of pleasure. Her intended apparently preferred that she put her waxing money toward their new home and that she pass her weekends with him rather than with Miss Michelle at Georgette Klinger's. Once again, it struck me, body hair was rearing its ugly head. This dentist asked in a moment of candor whether I thought she was doing the right thing. How much should she compromise? Marriage was entirely new to her, and she was certainly willing to try hard to make it work. But then she whispered, "Don't you draw the line at body hair?"

For myself, I leave it all to whimsy and mood swings. Sometimes I impulsively decide to spend an afternoon (well, half an hour, tops) with Miss Michelle. Other times I just completely forget about body hair—until it's time to go to the beach or give in and take a pail into the shower. As for the dentist's dilemma, I don't know the answer but I do have a hunch. When body hair becomes an issue, there's generally something far more substantial at stake.

The Messiah

y friend Vivian keeps a list of women past the age of thirty-five who decide to have a child, sleep with their
significant other, and—presto—nine
months later send out the pink or blue announcement
cards. Such success stories remind me of a certain camp
song we were admonished never, ever to sing. (Therefore
I remember the lyric in its entirety.)

Down by the station where nobody goes
Stands that Gladys without any clothes.
Along comes Alex swinging a chain,
Opened his zipper and out it came.
Three months later she wasn't feeling well,
Six months later started to swell.

Nine months later out they came
Six little Alexes swinging a chain.

To my friend Vivian, the swinging-a-chain song is more sentimental than "I'll Be Loving You Always."

These days the name of Sami David, M.D., is on everybody's lips. It seems that every time I have lunch with a friend I find out a little more. He's a prophet, a sage, a poet, a priest. He's the answer to every mid-thirtyish woman's prayers. He's Frank Sinatra, the Beatles, Bobby Kennedy, Allen Ginsberg, Kareem Abdul-Jabbar, and Dr. Salk all rolled into one. Over grilled radicchio at Bice and breakfast scones at Sarabeth's Kitchen there's hardly a chance encounter between two childbearing-age women where his name isn't brought up with a sigh. "Have you seen Dr. Sami David? He helped my friend." "If it wasn't for Dr. Sami, I don't know what I would have done." "Call Sami David. He's the best." And I don't mean Junior.

A friend of mine who several years ago became one of the first women partners at a major New York law firm once told me that she spent her twenties establishing her career and her thirties working to get pregnant. She's had numerous miscarriages, and vows to adopt by the time she's forty. In fact, most of my friends wouldn't dream of announcing they were PG until the fifth month. They don't want to share their happiness before the odds are in their favor that they'll get what they're entitled to. Theirs are decidedly mixed expectations.

I have listened to all the medical explanations—none of which, frankly, I can follow very well. An actress suddenly becomes an expert on reproduction—the egg was

here, the tube was there. An English professor re-
searches with insatiable gusto every new path possibly
open to her—an in vitro unit in Port Chester, a fertility
expert in Minnesota.

But the loss chips away. There is profound sadness
and regret in our acknowledging the existence of a force
—be it chemical, happenstantial, or genetic—that is beyond our control. We are a Filofaxed generation. Every
appointment, motivation, career move, even relationship
is carefully tabbed and structured. Most of the things my
friends want in their lives will eventually come to pass
through hard work, perseverance, and, all right, privilege. Our lives are not totally random. We make commit-
ments, we cause things to happen.

What concerns me is the unrevealed depths of the
pain and loss that my mid-thirtyish friends feel when they
fail to conceive or when they miscarry. Most of them
don't readily divulge their true feelings. They tend not to
say much and just keep on trying, citing the example of
another friend, someone who has recently been rewarded
with a six- or seven-pound happy ending. But at just
about every one of my Dr. Sami lunches, from Santa
Monica to London, at some point before we order the
decaf, a friend confides, "I wish I'd known about this a
lot sooner."

So what scares me most about the ascendancy of Dr.
Sami is not Dr. Sami himself. Hardly. I hear he's great.
Wonder of wonders, miracle of miracles. But what if the
hope for the prowess of Dr. Sami comes coupled with a
gnawing sense of guilt and resentment? In other words,
I fear that even my most clearheaded and open-minded
friends believe on some level that their difficulty, this
unexpected snag in an otherwise successful life, could
have been avoided if they hadn't for so many years pur-

sued independent lives. And the pressure to make up for lost time mounts accordingly. Babies or bust.

In 1969 the Junior Show at Mount Holyoke College, a musical extravaganza acted, written, and produced by the junior class, featured a finale in which the entire cast belted out "Suburbia Screw!" The anthem put a stunning end to the decade and to the school's unofficial motto, "Smith is to bed, Holyoke is to wed." The class of '69 had no intention of waking up from a marriage at forty-five, abandoned in a Scarsdale kitchen, with the kids in college and with a vague interest in Bernini. The class of '69 heard what Betty, Kate, and Germaine had to say. There were choices to be made, priorities to be weighed.

By and large the choices made were similar to my lawyer friend's—establish a career in the mid- to late twenties, put off childbearing until the mid-thirties. Those who set out to "screw suburbia" eventually became doctors, lawyers, and producers with enough clout to turn suburbia into a matter of real estate, a place to live, not manifest destiny.

In a single generation these women had radically altered the role of women in American society. The kitchen to which their forebears had seemed shackled was gradually transformed into a quick stop for a microwaved potato during the week and, on weekends, a cozy corner for drinks with an enlightened significant other, the prelude to a mutually prepared gourmet meal. Once this transformation took permanent hold, it became time to reproduce. But that's also when the doubts started.

Suddenly Mother, who at thirty-two had blithely driven around Winnetka with four kids and a golden retriever in the backseat of a station wagon, no longer seemed a deprived person. She seemed fortunate. Even blessed. And she had done it all, by and large, without even thinking. By the age of forty, just when her daughters were seeking the aid of Dr. Sami, Mother's work was nearly done and it was time to start traveling and seeing the world. I can't help feeling that some members of that 1969 junior class at Mount Holyoke who once believed that suburbia was screwed now secretly believe that they were, too.

I don't have a fifty-years-at-a-glance calendar, and I mostly disregard the tremors of the biological clock. I know mine is ticking; I have no idea for what date my alarm is set. When I was twenty-eight, a hot marital contender told me that I must choose between him and my play going to Broadway. My play didn't get to the Great White Way, but he and I certainly didn't make it to the altar either. I never deliberately set out to choose career over marriage and family. But my concentration span is limited. At best I can do two things at a time, and when they're finished I move on to the next. The problem with this philosophy of life is that it's based on time plodding along slower than sound, light, or even a stroll. No wonder my favorite fable is "The Tortoise and the Hare." Slow and steady wins the race.

Recently I've been unable to resist buying *People* magazine every time Mia Farrow, Glenn Close, or any other fortyish woman has a baby. A friend of my sister's just had her first child at fifty. I bet she got a truckload of layettes from anonymous well-wishers. I know I was tempted.

Oddly enough, I suspect that my being a Bachelor Girl has a lot to do with my hearing so many Dr. Sami stories.

It is what makes me, in a way, a safe harbor. There's an unspoken agreement between me and my friends that I won't judge them and they won't judge me. I can't be expected to understand completely my lawyer friend's initial joy at finding out she's pregnant, or her sense of grief and loss when she miscarries.

But even if I haven't coped with that kind of reality, I do empathize. And what saddens me deeply is that any of us should feel privately inadequate or deserving of judgment: me for the road so far not taken, my friends for the unexpected hazards and detours in their road. The self-recrimination for not being a certain kind of woman, a certain kind of mother, a certain kind of complete person is a quiet but constant undertow, a persistent dull ache. I wish all my friends could accept how fine and admirable they really are. I wish we could all offer ourselves such critical kindess. Anxiety screw!

As some of my mid-thirtyish friends begin their families, it will be as simple as the old swinging-a-chain song. But for others it will not be so easy. For their sake I hope all the stories I hear about Dr. Sami are true. I hope he can walk on water. I have his office and home numbers if you need them.

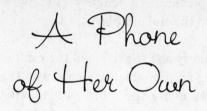

A Phone of Her Own

Something terrible has happened. It's not altogether a shock. I've had my suspicions for a while now. But looking back on the years of love, devotion, and even money that went into our now defunct relationship, I feel a loss, a gray April in my soul. My best friend, my interpreter and lifeline, has become my enemy. The thing I longed for as a teenager is now an object of neglect and scorn. I've grown to hate my telephone.

Apart from midwinter strolls on calm, starry nights, rolling over on a four-poster featherbed to reach for a beloved, and secretly indulging in a bottle of Fortnum & Mason hot fudge sauce, there has always been for me one unmitigated pleasure: a lengthy chat by phone. What the violin is to the Suzuki player, the telephone has been for me.

At a very early age, I perfected the craft of dialing "O"—summoning an invisible playmate was that simple. In fact, I asked so many operators whether they would play with me that my mother encouraged me to try Information—411—just for variety.

Whereas other children I knew got bored or anxious when their mothers chatted endlessly to unseen aunts and relatives, I found it hard to resist picking up the extension and jumping right in. Mid-juicy-conversation with my mother, my aunt Betty would pause to ask, "Wendy, honey, is that you on the line?" Being an honest child, I would answer, "Yes," and hang up the phone. Until next time.

Confidentially, when I, or rather the operators of the greater metropolitan area, tired of my calls, I matured and switched to the classic "Do you have Prince Albert in a can?" grocery store calls. Other favorites from this nuisance period include random calls to private homes. "Hello, this is the electric company. We're conducting a test. Please turn out all your lights. Are they out now? Dark, isn't it?" What I never understood was why anyone would think that a hysterically giggling nine-year-old was a spokesperson for Con Edison.

My true love affair, verging on obsession, began, however, when I realized that this two-part apparatus wasn't only for grown-up conversations or for playing games. My life-transforming discovery was that with a phone in the house you never really had to say goodbye to your friends at the bus stop. Arriving home from school, I would routinely announce, "Oh, hello, Mother. I promised Susan I'd call her." There was, after all, so much to discuss.

Such as why Sherry Hershman was becoming best friends with Nancy, the most popular girl in the class. And did Nancy, the most popular girl in the class, actually like Sherry or was she just using her to consolidate her popularity? These were pressing issues.

By high school most of us were learning foreign languages—among them the social graces and the facts of life. The latter included the extreme importance of telephone etiquette in the modern world (as demonstrated in that seminal communications work, the telephone song from the musical *Bye Bye Birdie*). In my teenage years, in New York City, boys didn't meet girls at county fairs or high school dances. The first connection was often by wire. "Hi, I sit behind you in Twentieth-Century Problems." Or "Hello. I got your name from my friend Rob, who goes to your camp." These initial calls were generally short and to the point. What took hours—and what was, frankly, much more pleasurable—was dissecting those initial calls with your best friend. "Why do you think he said 'Twentieth-Century Problems'? Does that mean he thinks we'll have problems?" "The way he said 'Hello' was pretty friendly. But I couldn't tell if he was just being polite or if he really likes me." These hours-long, line-monopolizing calls were so essential that a girl could hardly go on making do with just an extension. She required privacy, her very own number, a phone of her own.

Tracking the actual time I clocked on the phone during high school, I believe that if I had put that energy somewhere else I might have been an Olympic ice skater or built twin rockets and won the Westinghouse Science Fair. Countless evenings began with my dialing a friend at around seven and ended with our completing our homework together by around eleven. On nights when a mysterious *he* might be calling, I would pass the time not talking on the phone but staring at it. My parents became so concerned about my telephone fixation that my mother developed a game called "Walkie Talkie" in which she would take the phone from my bedroom, put it in her pocketbook, and walk—right out of the house.

My college days were spent in phoneless dorm rooms. Out of desperation, I soon became a regular on the pay phone circuit. There's no experience quite like squatting on the floor of a phone booth, smoking a cigarette, and crying about not getting into law school. At my alma mater, when a man called on the pay phone that served the entire floor of the dormitory, triumphant shouts would pour down the hall. "Wendy, male L.D.! Male L.D. for Wendy!" Ecstatically, I'd slide the length of the hallway—a home run! Long distance!

My feelings about the telephone began to change slightly, just slightly, when it came time to take responsibility for a phone of my own. First of all, since phones are a basic, like talking and eating, I have always believed they should be free. Moreover, the realization that most of the world uses the phone for practical purposes rather than for recreation is one of those bitter adult-passage adjustments we all have to make. Anyone who has ever had an entry-level job can tell you that personal calls are discouraged in the workplace. One of my least favorite supervisors once said to me as I began dialing, "You've already made one call today. And you've been to the bathroom twice!"

But for me the real essence of telephone ambivalence is connected to the answering machine. It's one thing to stare at the phone waiting for good news to ring, but another thing *never ever* to miss a single call. The possibilities for rejection are enormous. The fantasy that "Maybe they called while I was out" is cruelly eliminated.

The answering machine creates a give-and-take social contract: phone tag. Anyone with a Record-a-Call is likely to become an unwilling player. For example, if five messages have been left by an undesirable caller, protocol would have it that the caller deserves a response. The focus of one's life becomes returning telephone calls. The home becomes as hectic as an office.

And now, of course, everything about the phone has become overwhelmingly complicated. What started as a simple seven-digit twirl now involves call-forwarding, call-waiting, speakerphones, ITT, MCI, and Sprint. The peace of our backyards has been interrupted with cellulars. Even airplanes, once a haven from telephonic distraction, now often feature individualized receivers.

To this day I still can't stay long by myself in a house or hotel without a phone. I feel cut off, shut out, deprived of even the possibility of communication. But lately, seeking peace and short-term solitude, I sometimes find myself unplugging the phone, turning off the answering machine. More and more I prefer to write letters or make arrangements so that my conversations can be conducted in person, face to face. Seeing and talking with a friend over dinner seems much more intimate than a talk on the phone could ever be.

A few years ago a Hollywood agent boasted to me that she gave "good phone." At that moment I knew that my life skill, my dependable source of comfort, my personal performance art had been irrevocably co-opted.

* * *

I remember most of my phone numbers. Cloverdale 8-4847, our family home in Flatbush; 889-8988, my first apartment in New York. Nowadays on a lazy Sunday I might call a friend just to chat. In fact, on most days I still look at the phone and think that if I can get just a little more work done, *then* I can dial. But often when the telephone rings now, when it disturbs the peace, invades the territory, I cringe. Oh, please make it stop. Make it go away!

Anyway, the truth is I've taken up a new distraction. A new connection between two points. When the phone started to become a hassle, I transferred my infatuation to Federal Express.

It thrills me that packages can be delivered in twenty-four hours. I love zooming into the FedEx office at 9:00 p.m. Friday in New York and having my package arrive in Los Angeles by 10:30 a.m. Saturday. I love that I can send anything—a book, a pair of shoes, a chocolate bar. The Federal Express agents are just as nice as the Directory Assistance operators my mother once encouraged me to call. And if the day ever arrives when I discover that Federal Express is not a toy, I plan to go shopping for a fax machine of my own.

Avenue
of the
Stars

Being an East Coaster, I've always considered it my right and duty to feel ambivalent about L.A. After three months of living there, transplanted New Yorkers invariably learn to drive, hire a personal trainer, and begin to insist that the food is actually better in Los Angeles. After six months, they return to New York for Christmas to see everyone and everything, and confide that they wish they could move back East but their work makes that impossible now. By the end of a year, a nascent L.A.er is fluent in the real estate prices in Santa Monica, knows the right maître d' at The Ivy, and can tell you how much Chris Columbus—the screenwriter, not the explorer—gets up front for a first draft.

I can't say that I'm not attracted to it all. There's

something to be said for living in a Marcus Welby–type house in Brentwood, or working in a local industry that rewards its top performers with annual incomes like those of Aaron Spelling or Esther Shapiro, the instigators of "Charlie's Angels" and "Dynasty," respectively. Moreover, every woman I know who's moved to L.A. in the past five years has returned to New York (to visit) at least three inches taller. But it was not until my most recent visit to Los Angeles that I think I finally caught a glimpse of the essence of that town. For a moment the city seemed still, like a Hockney landscape—cold, bright, and dazzling.

I leave New York at 9 a.m. and arrive at LAX at 11:29. A car is to pick me up and whisk me to The Four Seasons hotel. (Apparently Canadians own The Four Seasons, a fact that in some people's minds makes the hotel preferable to the Sultan of Brunei's Beverly Hills Hotel or the recently renovated, Hong Kong–financed Regent Beverly Wilshire.) But since my plane has not arrived on schedule, there is no friendly driver holding my name scribbled on a piece of cardboard waiting to greet me. And so, New Yorker that I am, I follow my primary instinct with regard to any travel mishap or inconvenience, be it on the French Riviera or in the Rocky Mountains. I raise one hand and wail, "Taxi!"

However, my haste in this case causes some bureaucratic waste. Upon arrival at the hotel, I am informed by an attendant at the front desk that not only did the driver show up at the airport and fail to find me, but the hotel has no reservation in my name, and my New York agent is hysterical because American Airlines also has no record of me. I explain to the front desk that I am me, clear up the confusion of the missing reservation, and promise the attendant that I will call my agent to calm her.

Immediately upon entering my room, I raid the minibar for 7-Up, spring water, granola bars, and macadamia nuts. Then I remember the diet I'm supposed to be on, bolt the minibar, and dial room service to order up Spa cuisine. The phone rings.

"Hello, Miss Vasserstein. This is Radio Free Europe."

My agents aren't sure I'm in L.A., my movie studio has no idea where I am, but Radio Free Europe has found me.

"Hello. We want to talk to you about Rumania." The man on the phone has read an article I wrote about accompanying my niece to a chess tournament in Rumania.

"Right now?" My mind is on Spa cuisine and phoning New York, not on Rumania. "I'm at The Four Seasons in Los Angeles." It suddenly occurs to me that someone has kidnapped the driver and meddled with my plane and hotel reservations. Maybe by nightfall I'll be in Bucharest.

"We want to talk now."

I am beyond disoriented. I can't help feeling that I'm in a James Bond movie and a maid with blades that eject from her shoes will soon enter the room. Better not open the door for that Spa cuisine.

"I'm sorry. Another time."

"But we have you now."

"I'm really sorry. Please call my agent." Who, luckily, doesn't know where I am.

The sun is glaring on the terrace beyond the sliding glass doors. The furniture in the hotel room reminds me of

Jane Seymour's house, which I saw once either on "Life-styles of the Rich and Famous" or in *Architectural Digest*. It's white, overstuffed, and aggressively L.A. provincial. I sit curled in a corner and begin to dial allies.

My friend Patti suggests that I take a car—in L.A. "a car" means a hired car and driver—to my 3 p.m. meeting. She tells me I sound too crazy to drive. But the truth is I always sound too crazy to drive. Driving is commonly the first problem you encounter in L.A.

The studio is a glass building in beautiful downtown Burbank. The facade reflects the bright sunlight like Robert Redford's aviator glasses.

"We love your play. But we have trouble with the main character, the second act, and the ending. However, we think it could be a great movie."

A very chic twenty-six-year-old woman, who's probably at least thirty-five, wearing an $800 T-shirt and a gold Rolex watch, is chain smoking. In the room with us are three others—two men and a woman, I think—who are reiterating the twenty-six-year-old's opinions and thus trying to impress her. They all love my play. They all have problems with it.

I am reminded concurrently of Nathanael West's *The Day of the Locust* and "Let's Make a Deal."

Behind Box Number One we can enter into a dialogue. "Yes, I see what you're saying. Uh huh. Uh huh. That's interesting." Which means I want to be paid for a second draft and I'm willing to jump bullets for it.

Behind Box Number Two I'm outta here and they hire someone else to take a meeting with them.

As in most difficult situations, when the way out isn't a taxi, politeness will generally suffice. I will make sure they want to invite me back. I will handle the situation with all the direct aplomb of Radio Free Europe.

"I definitely see what you're saying. Let me think about it."

That night I take a walk from The Four Seasons into Beverly Hills. Walking is a defiant act in L.A. Jogging is for health, speedwalking is a remnant of a week at La Costa, but walking—strolling—is an Eastern urban excess.

I pass by La Petite Hermitage and try to peek through the lace curtains. I again can't remember whether I read it in *Architectural Digest* or saw it on "Lifestyles of the Rich and Famous," but the hotel is supposedly a popular recovery stop after that much-wanted cheek lift or tummy tuck. Lately I've been planning a weekend at a spa with my college roommate to celebrate her fortieth birthday. I can't help wondering whether we'll be checking in to La Petite Hermitage for her fiftieth.

It's eight o'clock and the light is fading on Rodeo Drive. Japanese tourists are still peering into the windows of Bijan and Pierre Deux. I approach a restaurant called The Grill. If chocolate cake could be grilled, it would be in L.A.—with extra virgin olive oil. My fondness for this particular place goes back to an opening night party for my play *Isn't It Romantic* at which the producers invited the entire cast of "Knots Landing" in the hope that we'd make "Entertainment Tonight." We didn't, but I got to meet Michelle Lee.

On this night The Grill is overrun not by series stars but by young women in tight off-the-shoulder black dresses and middle-aged TV executives with turquoise belts hugging their well-toned waistbands. No grilled tuna seems worth it. I decide to head home.

My taxi driver is Iranian and asks me for directions. I

can't believe I've been coming to this city for so long that I can find Doheny Drive.

Whenever I visit L.A., the first day I'm there I think the streets are paved with sit-coms and I should concentrate and come up with the premise for a new "Cosby Show." By the second day I decide to get really serious and work on becoming Morgan Fairchild. Inevitably, I make an appointment to see Olga, a Russian manicurist at Elizabeth Arden.

Olga moved to L.A. two years ago from Brighton Beach. So we schmooze about New York, what she misses, the people here, the people there. Olga hasn't grown three inches. She doesn't call everyone "honey" or "babe." She has no idea how much Chris Columbus gets for a screenplay. Olga's still a foreigner like me.

I had called my friend Peter a few days earlier to tell him I was coming to L.A. for the weekend, and he'd informed me that he was going back into the hospital for a tune-up. Just a look-see clearing up of his lungs. When I phone again on Saturday morning, he asks me to visit in the late afternoon, when he thinks he won't be busy.

Peter has AIDS. His blood type is listed in his Filofax as "immune deficient." Five months ago my friend Patti and I had attended Peter's Two Years and Still Kicking party. This time Patti has offered to drive me to see Peter in the hospital.

I tell Patti I'm loose until the late afternoon. So we visit the Bruno Magli selection at the shoe salon at Neiman Marcus, the greatest variety of colors and sizes I know of in the nation. I invest in a pair of taffeta slippers and some evening pumps, and Patti and I cruise on to the Beverly Center Cineplex.

I love seeing movies in L.A. Mostly because everyone who is anyone has already seen them at a screening. Patti and I sit through the two o'clock showing of *Scandal* next to a woman who is dressed as Morticia on "The Addams Family."

Around four-thirty we set off for the hospital. I make a quick stop to buy a lily plant and we're on our way. The Century City Hospital also looks like Robert Redford's sunglasses. Patti says she'll come back to pick me up in an hour.

I ride the elevator to the fourth floor. There are CAUTION signs, warnings, posters with construction-paper flowers, and sunshine. The corridor is bright, sun-filled. No one stops me. A young man in hospital whites is seated behind a desk. He smiles at me. I smile at him and proceed to Peter's room.

I always had a crush on Peter. He seemed the epitome of the well-bred East Coast gentleman—and he had a sense of humor about it. He was handsome, Andover and Yale, a man familiar with shingle-style architecture, Benjamin Britten's operas, and the complete literature of Bloomsbury. The year Peter starred in *Children of a Lesser God,* he would giggle with me about the matinee ladies who came to see him in "Amadeus of a Much Lesser God."

Peter and I were born in the same year, 1950, and now he was thinking of writing his memoirs, his life in the theater. It wouldn't be half as long a memoir as he deserved. And it would have an incongruous ending. Many of Peter's waking hours were now devoted to doing crosswords and watching daytime television.

Peter is breathing into a plastic pipe and coughing

into a plate when I peek into the room. I smile as though I don't notice. Peter says they haven't finished with his treatment.

"Oh, I'll come back. I'll take a meeting. I'll have a power coffee." Peter laughs and coughs again. I squeeze his foot and leave the room.

Century City is deserted Saturday late afternoon. The Rolex-watch girls at ABC and CAA are home exercising, reading hot screenplays, and spending quality time with their families. The office buildings become wedges of light. A tunnel for the brightness to pass through.

I begin running toward the Century Plaza Hotel across the Avenue of the Stars. I can't make any sense out of it. What are Peter and I doing here? Why is he dying in a hospital in L.A.? And how have I come to know so much about this city I'm so suspicious of? As I run, the light becomes brighter and brighter. The glare is stunning. At this moment I understand. Peter and I are Easterners who have come West. Like so many other people, we have been drawn here by the promise of a certain freedom—the comfort of *not* belonging, the chance to reinvent ourselves. But, unlike those who stay so long that they learn to live entirely for the present moment and repress their past lives, we plan to go back home at the end of the ride, and have always just assumed that we could.

Thirty minutes later I return to see Peter. The pipe is gone. But he looks thinner, frailer. He's been hoping to be in a friend's movie that is scheduled to begin filming next month in New York. But he has just found out that the casting director won't consider the risk of hiring an actor with AIDS.

As he tells me this story, Peter's eyes fill with tears. "It's so unfair!" Until this moment I have never seen

Peter complain about his illness. I'm sure he has complained, but not to me. He would never impose. He is too much of an East Coast gentleman.

That evening Patti and I drive up and down the Santa Monica Strip. We blast the oldies radio station and call everyone we know from Patti's car phone. This is the L.A. we fantasized about as girls back East. Cars, the radio, and surfer boys. This is the L.A. we dreamed of long before we knew about three-picture deals, development girls, or Bruno Magli shoes.

Patti and I pull into DC 10, the hip place of the moment, in the old Santa Monica airport. Here again are the girls in black, the TV executives, and fish, vegetables, and minerals all grilled with extra virgin olive oil.

A chill goes through me. It is likely that I will never see Peter again. But I will be back here. And, strangely, my memory of Peter—his tweed jackets, Bloomsbury books, and Off-Broadway triumphs—will become inextricably attached to this too-light and too-fast West Coast city.

In
Charm's
Way

In that seminal classic of "American Bachelor Girls on the Town" cinema, *How to Marry a Millionaire,* there's a pivotal scene in which Betty Grable brings home to Lauren Bacall and Marilyn Monroe a real nice oil fella she met in the fur department of Bergdorf's. Betty enters the apartment with at least twenty simply divine purple boxes with those just adorable black-figurine diagonal stripes. The oil fella trails behind her. Left to the viewer's imagination is Betty's and the fella's actual spree at the fur salon. Did she point as she said, "I'll take this and that, and that and this, and this!"? Or did she try on each coat and pose in the mirror while the White Russian émigré princess saleslady winked, "She looks vonderful in all of them. How can you choose?"

Well, gals, I've got a hot tip for you. Forget the fur department fantasy. It's unkind to animals and, besides, you can do better. A Fendi fox might be quite continental, but it ain't a Picasso. Betty, Marilyn, and Lauren were fifties kinds of gals with fifties kinds of fantasies. Those of us who have survived changing our names from "Miss" to "Ms." and "Mrs." and back again deserve something a little more substantial—like a Matisse. I promise you there is nothing like walking through the Lila Acheson Wallace Wing of 20th-Century Art at the Metropolitan Museum of Art with museum director Philippe de Montebello as your guide, and fantasizing a spree amid the Picassos, Matisses, and Chagalls. "Philippe, or may I call you Monty? I'll take this and that, and that and this, and this!" Trust me. It's a lift.

The odds that I would ever call Philippe de Montebello "Monty" are about equal to the odds that I'd win a Distinguished Achievement in Modern Medicine award for gene splicing, or go Christmas shopping at Toys "Я" Us with Raisa Gorbachev. In fact, our proposed luncheon brought on a variety-pack of anxieties, both personal and cultural. My fears included, "In Baroque paintings, does the light flood in from the right or the left?" "Do salads make too much noise?" And "Oh God, I hope I don't quote from Janson's *History of Art.*"

In a state of pre-lunch trauma I sought the counsel of cultivated friends. "He's very nice to his curators," one offered. Another smirked, "Are you familiar with the lyric from *My Fair Lady,* 'oozing charm from every pore, he oiled his way across the floor'?" And a final helpful hint: "Philippe's ancestors arrived in France before the *saucisson.*" All right, so we weren't going to turn out to be related. And I'm certainly no curator, so I couldn't be assured of his being nice. That left oozing charm. "Oh please, God, don't let him pull out a chair for me just as I'm sitting down in the wrong one." Charm can be so disorienting.

I arrive at the information desk at the Met. "Hello. I have a lunch appointment with the director."

"The museum shop is to your right."

Not really. A nice museum lady wearing a silk shirt and a nice scarf calls to announce my arrival, then writes out a pass. "Through the Greek and Roman. Take the elevator to the mezzanine, and the executive offices are just down the corridor."

A word about the Metropolitan. It's usually full of life, and that day was no exception—nice ladies in scarves, art students, older couples, schoolchildren, tourists (Italian-speaking, Spanish-speaking, even British). As I walked through the Greek and Roman permanent collection, I couldn't help thinking back on our Latin-class field trips. Fall semester we came to see the kithara player, the babe with the brown eyes on the fading red wall—proof that Roman art was equal to Greek art. Spring semester we came to see the giant head of Constantine—proof that Roman art was never equal to Greek.

They were still there. The greatest hits from around the world and across the centuries. Suddenly the prospect of lunch seemed simple. Well, simpler. Like most of the people there, I had and will continue to have a long-term relationship with the museum. Sometimes we might not see each other for years. But I know that I can depend on it—it is always stimulating and embracing. And so it was that day. Functioning like a great. I was actually beginning to look forward to meeting Philippe.

Philippe de Montebello is, as my mother would say, *takesh* (very) handsome. (The odds that I would tell him *that* are even less than the "Monty" odds.) He shakes my hand in his book-lined office. I look him over: groomed dark hair, steel blue eyes, a perfectly tailored houndstooth suit and blue Hermès tie. He looks me over and, as he does, I hope that he notices the Bruno Magli alligator pumps and not the $45 Eighth Street dress. He seems entirely at ease. I mean, after all, there isn't a Wendy Wing at stake.

As we leave his office, he tells his assistant that if so-and-so calls, "I'm not going to Argentina this weekend."

I smile. "Were you planning to go to Argentina this weekend?"

"Yes, but my son is getting married."

"How old is your son?"

"Twenty-two."

So, we're chatting.

The executive, hotsy-totsy, museum-members-only dining room at the Met is a small, pleasant room just east of the less hotsy-totsy, fountained visitors' galley. People definitely take notice of us as we enter. I'm hoping the four young gentlemen to our right think I'm some very important avant garde—type from Avenue D.

We order drinks. A white wine for me, just in case we get into my opinions on Poussin, and tomato juice for him.

"So, you're here to find out about the real Philippe de Montebello," he says.

Nobody says "de Montebello" the way Philippe does. The inflection is perfect. Not too much. The delivery is never forced. But there's a basso on the "bello." In fact, Philippe's accent is *takesh* perfect. Van Gogh is pronounced "van Gogue." Delacroix buttons with a staccato "croi," with nary a trace of an "x." It's no wonder the director's recorded cassette tours are *the* "in" accessory in the Impressionists wing. As Philippe himself admits, "They used to call me the eyes. Now they call me the voice."

The director and I continue chatting about his children. His son is marrying a French girl, and they'll be moving in with him temporarily. He's already trying to help them find housing of their own that they can afford. I suggest Phipps Houses Services—a middle-income project I lived in when I first came back to New York after graduate school. He writes the name down on the inside of a matchbook. Is this the real Philippe de Montebello?

We order lunch. He has an omelette with *pommes frites.* I have a chicken salad. (The mayonnaise will diminish the volume of the crunch.) A woman in her sixties sporting a rhinestone "Paris" pin on her turtleneck sashays up to our table. With her is a younger, very chic-looking sixteenth-arrondissement French woman in regulation Chanel suit and black velvet hair bow.

The older woman begins, "Oh Mister de Montebello, I hate to disturb you, but my friend just had to meet you. She knows your relatives." Aha, another pre-*saucissoner!* My lunch companion smiles and breaks into, of course, perfect French. After les mademoiselles leave the table, Philippe (we're intimate now) confesses to me that he has no idea who either of them is, and, furthermore, the woman's friends are related not to him but to his son's fiancée.

I sip the wine. I sip the water. I cover a pause. "Do

you spend a lot of your time talking to ladies like that? I mean, do you spend a lot of your time fund-raising, or do you have a development office? (No, it rains Velásquez from heaven.)

Philippe explains that of course when one is dealing with grants and large donations, people "want to see the real thing. But," he continues, "I rather enjoy fund-raising, because I am speaking about something I have a passion for. And I am actually very good at it."

"Do you get competitive with other institutions?"

"Not really. A person could see me and Jimmy Levine in the same day. But it's not competitive. And most have their favorites, their passions. The problem is I have to see so many people that when I have a free night in New York, I tend to spend it at home. So I go to concerts when I am in London, Paris, or Vienna."

Our lunch arrives. The chicken salad is silent. For some reason we begin talking about the Marxist orientation of Harvard's art history department. He explains, "For instance, they can look at a haystack in a painting by Cézanne and interpret it as Cézanne's plea for the plight of the workers. And of course they all love Corot." Of course. I mention something about socialist realism and content over form. I'm pulling it out from a hazily remembered sophomore-year art history lecture. That's when I realize he is "actually very good at it." He makes me feel comfortable. He makes me feel that he is interested in what I have to say. He makes me feel that he could happily spend an entire afternoon listening to me prattle on about art.

Another pause. Another sip. All right, it's sentimental, but I decide to tell him how wonderful it was coming into the museum and seeing it so full of life. He smiles and says, "And it's only a weekday." Philippe de Montebello is an artistic director and, like any artistic director of a great cultural institution, he is proud, protective, and opinionated, in a tasteful way. "Have you been to the Philadelphia Museum?" he asks me. "Oh, it's a wonderful museum, but it's empty. And in Chicago they go only to see the Impressionists. The one museum that is really crowded is the East Wing of the National Gallery. And the crowds there are all for those special shows. The West Wing, the Baroque Galleries, are empty! But that's show business."

Show business. Now we're talking. Kinda like colleagues.

"Can you say something is less good because it's popular?" he asks me. "Who would say an in-depth study of van Gogh is simply popular?"

Say *van Gogue* again! Please!

"If I have to choose between an exhibit of Delacroix and Corinthian vases . . ." (N.B. At this point I'm not sure whether he's said Corinthian, Cornucopian, or Conniption vases, but I continue to smile) ". . . do I do the Delacroix, which will be more popular, or the C—— vases, because it will be an important exhibit, a first?"

I'm feeling very included. I'm loving this lunch. "Oh, well," I say, smiling, "the only art form I know of for which being popular is congruent to being aesthetic is the American musical—like *South Pacific*." Just when I'm loving it, I push it over the edge. Another sip—water, wine. Forget *Oklahoma!*, let's have coffee. The real Philippe de Montebello likes to stay on his own turf.

Two double espressos. He tells the waiter that he may have the Black Forest cake sent up to his office at four o'clock.

"Are you supposed to interview me?" he asks. It's

true, I haven't been taking notes or taping. Just chewing quietly.

"No," I giggle. "We're supposed to have a lovely lunch." I decide to move on. "Do you have tenure here?"

"No. I'm at the mercy of my board. But I hope to stay at least six more years. I'm hoping to put my youngest son through college, and possibly then move back to France. And I'm writing a book."

The book is his personal guide to his favorite and least favorite paintings throughout the world. He confides: "Publishing this sort of book, it helps if you are still the museum director." He smiles. The smile isn't warm, but it's debonair. I have no idea what he's really thinking.

Then he pays the bill. We've done it.

"Is there anything else I can show you?"

"Of course." I want the dirt. "Can I see your least favorite painting here?"

We walk through the plebeian galley. He points to a mural on the wall. "That was from the *Normandie*." Nobody ends "Normandie" with a "dee" the way Philippe does.

Halfway through the Greeks and Romans, he changes his mind. It wouldn't be right to show me his least favorite painting. He will show me something even better. He will take me to the new Lila Acheson Wallace Wing of 20th-Century Art, which on this day of our lunch has not yet been opened to the public.

Passing through the galleries, we encounter a group of rowdy young public-school students. Philippe quips, "Sometimes I wonder if they really get anything out of this place." For a moment, I am reminded of the *My Fair Lady* lyric.

As we approach the new wing I mention that Barnabas McHenry, the former chief executor of the Lila Wallace Foundation, is a friend of mine. Once again we are on equal ground. There is a link between the theater and the art worlds. We agree that Barney is a visionary arts funder. But I wonder in passing why I have dropped his name to Philippe. Perhaps because Barney works so hard in service of his dream that those kids will get something out of this place.

The wing is staggering. Light playing amongst the Picassos. Philippe offers that the museum's goal is for the galleries to be inviting, not stark. I smile at a Rothko, and move on to the Pollacks, and a spectrum of Ellsworth Kelly. Philippe is proud. "A person can now have a full experience at the Metropolitan." I think, You mean from Latin class and the bust of Constantine to today and Matisse with you.

Now, girls, here's where he gets so much better than the oil fella. And forget about those Marxists at the Harvard art history department.

We pass a pastel Manhattan cityscape. "That's Union Square, isn't it?" Philippe asks me.

"Uh huh. That's Klein's." I smile. "I think it's a Fairfield Porter," I add.

Philippe's fairly excited. "Is that a Fairfield Porter? Let's see."

We go over to the painting. He lifts it off the wall. "I can't see. Can you read it?"

"Yes." I actually hold the painting in my hands. "It's a Fairfield Porter."

How could he possibly know that holding that painting would give me as great a thrill as stroking that mink gave Betty Grable? And does it matter if it was all just charm? If I had a million dollars, I'd donate a Wendy Wing.

* * *

Philippe de Montebello drops me off at the Treasures of the Holy Land exhibit. We shake hands. He tells me to see the exhibit if I haven't already, and that is it. *Au revoir,* Philippe. The Red Seas part, leaving behind only the de Montebello Walkman guide to the Holy Land.

"Monty, I'll take the Dead Sea scrolls, the fourth-century B.C. earrings, the Pontius Pilate inscriptions, and the fourteenth-century B.C. cult mask."

Not really. They should stay right here. For everyone to visit and enjoy.

On my way out, I stop by to say hello to *Aristotle Contemplating the Bust of Homer.* Mister de Montebello, with the basso on the "bello," you run a wonderful place. Much better than the fur department at Bergdorf's.

Mrs. Smith Goes to Washington

There are days when I can't help thinking about Geraldine. I think about the moment she accepted her nomination. I think about where I was, who I was with, and why it made me cry. It was very simple: Finally, one of *us* was there. Whatever had happened in all of our lives —careers, babies, marriage, no careers, no babies, no marriage—was all on a much larger scale of significance. Geraldine, up there, meant there'd been some changes made.

In 1988 as I watched them all—Bush, Dole, Jackson, Dukakis, Gephardt, Gary (I feel all women have the right to be on a first-name basis with Gary)—I kept wondering, Where's the one who's up there for us? It reminded me of the Eisenhower years, when I'd watch the news on TV and wonder, Why aren't there any girls? And it didn't look like much fun to be Mamie.

Yes, I read the reports in all the newsweeklies that there is a new breed of political wife. They no longer wear cloth coats and retreat to their private rooms in desolation. They are attractive team players with law degrees of their own and they raise attractive, sports-minded children. They are separate but equal partners, even former Cabinet members. I can't help wondering if at this point, after the fallout from Geraldine, the only one of us who could be up there is a well-schooled, well-balanced, well-figured team player.

My sister's favorite political figure in 1988 was Elizabeth Hanford Dole. Liddy is the ideal wife. She's beautiful, she has a very successful career, and she's evidently willing to put it on hold for her husband. Geraldine was a pushy Queens housewife who gave up her career only when her husband was potentially on the descent. But Liddy made the grand sacrifice. She denied herself for her husband's potential. Bravo, Liddy.

Actually, I don't mean to be snide. I admire Liddy Dole. She has great charm and probably—if I knew more about her than what the news media offer—intelligence. What troubles me is the message that Liddy, Tipper Gore, and the other "new" political wives are sending not just to my sister but to a new generation of women.

A few years ago I was invited back to my college, Mount Holyoke, to see a production of my play *Uncommon Women and Others*. The play is about five college seniors in the seventies who, faced with the real world, explore their feelings about marriage and careers versus their background in tea and gracious living.

When I arrived at the school several of the students told me how much they liked my play even though it was "a period piece." I could barely refrain from saying, "Who do you think I am, Sheridan?" When I asked them to explain what they mean by "period," they said, "Well, the women at your time were so confused about sex and graduate school. We're not confused. We know we're going to professional school, and we know all about sex."

In *Uncommon Women* there is a wistful refrain: "When we're forty we'll be pretty amazing." These students, most of them only twenty years old, seemed both competent and confident—already pretty amazing. In fact, most of them already had life plans mapped out. Blue for long-term personal goals, red for short-term career decisions.

But if this new generation of women allows itself to be guided by the fallout from Geraldine and the example of Liddy, then for them being "pretty amazing" will be equivalent to keeping everything in line—success in moderation. And I wonder what will happen to those students who now seem so secure, so certain, when they discover that a piece of the pie doesn't fit. What happens if they stray out of the norm and life gets messy, unbalanced just a bit? When such an enormous effort is invested in being the common denominator—being all desirable things to all desirable people—there is very little room for a real personal agenda.

Maybe the reason I keep thinking about Geraldine is that when she approached the podium we were all up there together—confident and unconfident students, single mothers, single nonmothers, nonworking mothers, single career women, working mothers. We were not the woman wearing the red suit, the pillbox hat, the three strands of pearls standing next to the man who, of course, did all the talking. We were not the tasteful arts advocate, the former beauty queen Harvard lawyer, or the white-haired grandmother who had managed to sustain marriage, family, 50,000 miles of air travel, and as a reward now got to wave madly before a crowd of her husband's admirers.

Whether you like Geraldine or not, her nomination said something about our times. It was historic. There was someone else up there waving, smiling, beaming proudly. Someone in *our* shoes. At that moment everything seemed perfectly clear, almost brilliant. Now things are blurry, splintered again.

But I do have hope.

About a year ago I received the following message on my telephone answering machine: "Hello, my name is Nita Lowey and I'm running for Congress in Westchester County. We have the same alma mater, and I was wondering if you'd care to meet me and have tea."

Tea with Nita was startling to me. She was around fifty years old, my sister's age, had graduated from Mount Holyoke, and then had married and started a family. Her early adult life had been spent as the wife of a lawyer and as a trooper for the PTA. Later she had moved from local community service to work in state government, and eventually became an Assistant Secretary of State in New York. Now she was ready to try her hand at elected office, to take on an incumbent. For Nita there seemed to be no pre-existing well-balanced plan. She had simply responded to an opportunity and made the decision to pursue a goal that she hoped passionately to achieve. And her attitude seemed to be that, if it didn't work out, at least there was something she deemed worthy of taking a risk, breaking out of the mold, getting a little dirty for. There was nothing moderate about her aspiration.

Six months later I accepted an invitation to attend a Women's Campaign Fund gathering. The fund raises money for women candidates regardless of party affiliation. Among the speakers at the event were Susan McLane, a State Senator from New Hampshire; Nancy Johnson, a Congresswoman from Connecticut; and Elizabeth Holtzman, the Brooklyn District Attorney who would later be elected Comptroller of the City of New York. As I listened to the speakers, each of them very different, I began to feel the same excitement that I felt on the day Geraldine accepted her nomination. Especially when, halfway through the festivities, my old friend Nita Lowey turned up. Mrs. Lowey, who since I'd last seen her had become a member of the United States Congress, smiled and waved as the audience applauded her remarks, and then, due to a hectic schedule, slipped away early to return to her office in Washington.

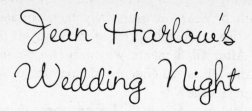

Jean Harlow's Wedding Night

man I was engaged to asked me to meet him in Paris. Credit Suisse was putting him up at the George V, he said, and wouldn't it be pleasant to spend a few evenings together?

Well, that's not really how the story goes. Actually, this banker I had been dating for two months was planning a business trip to Paris. I knew that New York would be unbearable without him since my career, my friends, my apartment, even my cat failed to provide me with a sense of fulfillment equal to what I felt in his company. So I managed after about three hundred phone calls, and after five days of putting all my other work on hold, to secure a writing assignment in Paris: "A Bachelor Girl's Guide to Paris in the Springtime," or whatever.

So that my banker friend wouldn't dare think I was in Paris just to be near him or that my magazine assignment wasn't my first priority, I arranged to stay at the Plaza-Athénée. After all, I mean, why would a person with a room at the Plaza-Athénée be desperate to spend the night at the George V?

Before my friend arrived, I spent three days in Paris thinking about him. I thought about him at the Musée Rodin, at the Jo Goldenberg delicatessen, and at a showing of *Back to the Future* with French subtitles. The day before he arrived I wrote him a note from Madame de Staël, which I ripped up; a note from Simone de Beauvoir, which I ripped up; notes from Empress Josephine, Marie Curie, Desiree, Simone Weil—all of which I ripped up. Finally, I composed a simple and discreet note from myself, and left it in an envelope with his name on it at the front desk at the George V.

My banker friend liked my note. He called to thank me for it and invited me over to see his hotel suite. We stayed together that night in Paris. We ordered up champagne and salmon steak, and my friend asked whether I would mind if he watched the soccer match on TV. I didn't mind. I'd been anticipating this moment for days. I could easily feign interest in those hyperactive men bobbing balls off their heads.

Eventually we went to bed. It was one of those torrid experiences when I wished I could be replaced by Debra Winger in *Urban Cowboy*. If only I could pretend he was the mechanical bull at Gilley's. If only I had that kind of stamina. I was completely and totally smitten.

At 6 a.m. I rolled over on the 38,000-thread cotton sheets and felt him gone. I looked across the room toward the gilded rococo desk—there sat my friend, wearing jogging shorts and a Duke University T-shirt, lacing up his Nikes. His lanky runner's body and his still youthful locks of curly hair shone in the morning light. I was convinced that I loved him more than any man I'd ever known.

I pulled a sheet around me and walked over to embrace him. I wanted him to know how very safe and protected he was with me, I wanted him to know that he didn't have to run away at 6 a.m. As I went to press my lips to his head, he smiled boyishly and looked up at me with his very smart and very dear dark brown eyes.

"Honey, I've met someone new."

Suddenly I became preposterously funny. I chatted on and on about the room service at the George *Cinq;* about the croissants, the waiter, the plates, anything that entered my mind. I had gotten as far as the Ayatollah Last Chance Diet when I finally made him smile. My hurt, my expectations, were none of his business. I wanted to keep the situation light. I wanted to keep it funny.

Most of the time I don't feel particularly amusing. This is odd only because if you asked almost anyone of my acquaintance to name my outstanding characteristics, the answer you'd get most often would be, "Oh, she's very funny."

As a child, given a Saturday afternoon choice between Audrey Hepburn getting kissed in Technicolor on the "Million Dollar Movie" and an "I Love Lucy" rerun in which Lucy and Ethel dress up yet again to perform at Ricky's Tropicana Club, I would invariably choose Lucy. I was one of those youngsters who cover their eyes and squeal "yuck" when in the end the boy gets the girl. Usually this was because the girl was so boring and what the boy loved about her was that she was so boring. If nothing else, Lucy and Ethel at least got to be lively. At least they were permitted to have runs in their stockings.

I first realized that other people found me funny when in the second grade, after careful practice, I brought down the classroom with my comedic routines on our prospects for lunch. (Vegetable Chop Suey was a highlight.) Through the next several years my satiric gifts allowed me to form alliances with rival "most popular girls in the class" because I was considered good company and had absolutely no interest in vying for their title. I was an elementary school Falstaff.

Being perceived as funny served me well even when it got me into trouble. My comments about Mrs. Haskell, our seventh-grade teacher, whom I was put on earth to single-handedly torture, were apparently so scathing that for an entire semester I was forced to stay after class two hours every day. But I didn't mind. I still arrived home in time for dinner, and I got a good early start on my homework.

Anyone who is considered funny will tell you, sometimes without your even asking, that deep inside they are very serious, neurotic, introspective people. In other words, Eddie Murphy has the heart of Hannah Arendt and Joan Rivers is really J. Robert Oppenheimer.

Personally I don't spend much time thinking about being funny. For me it's always been just a way to get by, a way to be likable yet to remain removed. When I speak up, it's not because I have any particular answers; rather, I have a desire to puncture the pretentiousness of those who seem so certain they do.

Therapists have on occasion told me to check my impulse to entertain—to stop being funny—and to allow my real emotions to surface. Sometimes this is helpful. But other times the ability to move beyond and above the sadness, even the tragedy, of a particular moment is one of life's greatest survival mechanisms. There is nothing even vaguely amusing about the truth of the Holocaust, about AIDS, or about the human race's capacity for self-annihilation. We should be grateful, then, that the minor mishaps of life, such as my ill-fated rendezvous with the banker, can be jostled into a wry position.

That morning in Paris I wasn't just funny; I was angry, I felt hurt, I had been misled. Of course, I blamed it all on myself. If only I had worn red instead of that floral print, or Opium rather than L'Heure Bleue. If only I had left the note from Madame de Staël.

Later, as my friend showered and got dressed, I joked that I'd better get back to writing that news-breaking magazine article, "No Sex and the Single Girl in Paris." There's nothing like a self-deprecating exit line to ease the pain of an unenchanted parting. That morning I could think of many other places I'd prefer to Paris in the springtime.

Usually, in fact, I do fall back on work. Work is a way of losing oneself that has plenty of advantages. Work is a way of shutting out ambiguous sentiment. Work is one way out of having to be preposterously funny. But work requires concentration, and, frankly, that morning I felt like Sputnik in orbit.

As a break from an afternoon of countless abortive beginnings, innumerable bottles of Perrier, and repeated rereading of *The International Herald Tribune,* I decided to call my banker friend at his office just to say hello. I wanted him to know that I was fine about it all, and that despite the failure of our romance I wanted to stay friends. Oh *please!*

"Hi," my voice squeaked in an unexplored octave. "Just calling to say hi."

All he said was yes. But it was that kind of "Dear Occupant" yes that one reserves for unsolicited magazine-subscription offers. The more distant he sounded, the stronger my compulsion to entertain.

Soon I was at full-tilt boogie. One-two-three anecdote. One-two-three anecdote. It was a good thing I didn't know any Chernobyl or Natalie Wood jokes or I would have pulled those out, too. Finally I blurted that if he wasn't busy or "like had finished his work," I had heard of this hilariously hip restaurant that was a favorite among radical deconstructionist Marxist Chanel models.

He laughed. I had broken through.

"I would love to." He was almost jovial. "But I have a previous engagement. Actually, right now I'm waiting for the party to call and confirm. Thank you for thinking of me."

If I were really the clever girl I pose as, I would have said, "You're welcome." Instead I let him go with a polite "Well, if your plans change let me know."

I immediately took a taxi to the Jeu de Paume. Fine, as long as I was in Paris I might as well be there for a better reason than a one-night stand with "Thank you for thinking of me." Despite this blow I was still a resourceful and sensitive person. This was apparent because in a time of turmoil I chose a museum over an impulsive shopping spree for, say, Hermès scarves—which, by the way, I don't really care for.

But no sooner had I arrived at the early Degas collection than I felt a darkness that wouldn't leave me. I found myself sitting in front of leaping pink horses and sobbing uncontrollably.

In the hope that a rush of endorphins would kick in and calm me down, I left the museum and, to avoid the stares of passersby, retreated to a corner of the Jardin des Tuileries. As I sat there sobbing amid the tourists, the dog walkers, and the students wearing backpacks, I felt as if I'd somehow come in touch with my true self. For a funny person, I felt frighteningly empty. And it wasn't because I was unlucky in love, alone in a foreign land, or overwhelmed by the beauty of great paintings; it was just me—plain, honest, and empty.

And as soon as I recognized this, I heaved another teary sigh and remembered that I had promised to call my friend Patti in New York to relay every sordid detail of my Paris sojourn. I decided I'd name the evening "Jean Harlow's Wedding Night" as a tip of the hat to Jean's unconsummated nuptials. The thought of recounting the story to Patti—from the Brazilian soccer match to the Duke T-shirt at 6 a.m.—cheered me up immensely. With a few minor nips and tucks, my account of the episode could make an amusing cautionary tale.

I wiped my face and went back to the Jeu de Paume. I even hummed a little Cole Porter on the way. I am, after all, a resourceful and sensitive person, and I love Paris in the springtime.

Christmas in Flatbush

I had never been inside a house with a Christmas tree until my freshman year at college. Then, one snowy New England night, a phalanx of caroling students decked out in Lanz flannel nightgowns surprised my roommate and me and urged us to grab our favorite teddy bears and join them to light the tree. The entire dormitory, 130 strong in Lanz flannel nightgowns, caroled in the living room as our housemother distributed gingerbread cookies and toys from our "secret Santas."

I silently wished that someone from my old neighborhood, Vince or Donna who hung out on "the highway" in front of the Avalon Theater in Flatbush, Brooklyn, could have witnessed this ritual. I wanted Donna, whose peroxide hair was teased to Olympus, or Vince, who must have used a shoe horn to squeeze not only into his Thom McAn twister boots but also into his skin-tight pants, to take a peek through our dormitory window.

"Hey, girlie," they'd have shrieked if they had seen us. "What are you doing in there? Where'd *you* learn to celebrate the holidays?"

During my Flatbush childhood, I was in awe of Christmas. I longed to have a reindeer climbing down my family's front porch and a life-size Santa twinkling on our lawn like the one on the corner of Ocean Parkway and Avenue U. I wanted my dad to wear a fading V-neck sweater and croon to us like Perry Como.

It wasn't that my family didn't celebrate Hanukkah. My mother played a mean dreidel, and there were potato latkes, gifts, and even an all-expenses-paid trip to the children's floor at Ohrbach's.

And, of course, at school every December we retold the story of the little can of oil, enough for one day, that burned for seven days and seven nights. Throughout those years I thought of that story as "The Little Can of Oil That Could."

Perhaps it was because, at the yeshiva in Flatbush, we never studied the religious aspects of Christmas, the holiday seemed to me spectacular, truly magical.

Whereas we got one Sunday morning public-television program about the Maccabees, they got *It's a Wonderful Life, Miracle on 34th Street,* plus the 24-hour burning Yule log. We got electric menorahs, they got a zillion-foot tree in Rockefeller Center and the Radio City Christmas show. In my mind, no spinning dreidel, even from Barton's Bonbonniere, could compare to the Rockettes.

* * *

Christmas in Flatbush really meant Christmas in Miami. There was no reason to stay home for the holidays. The point of Christmas, as far as my parents were concerned, was peace-on-earth-good-will-to-men and to get the whole family on a Pullman to Florida.

In the Miami Beach of the late 1950s, Christmas was hardly apparent except in the twinkling white trees that decorated the lower lobby of the Fontainebleau Hotel. The holidays were a time for the family to catch Harry Belafonte at the Diplomat, build sand castles on the beach, avoid jellyfish, and dance with Dad under the stars to a Latin combo.

My most vivid Christmas Day memories are of my brother and sister searching out frozen Milky Ways at the Rexall drugstore on Collins Avenue. This hardly compares, I suppose, with unwrapping Grampa's gift by the warming fire or under the mistletoe. But we were all together then, and I remember those days more than fondly.

My first real Christmas was, suitably, in Oxford, England. I was visiting the home of a friend's brother who was studying to be a theologian in the Anglican Church.

For weeks before my trip, I consulted friends about what gifts to bring and about which ensembles were most appropriate for Christmas Eve as opposed to Day. I was reluctant to let on to the aspiring deacon that my religious training to date consisted primarily of watching the Radio City Christmas show and caroling at Mount Holyoke in my nightie.

That evening in Oxford we ate lobster Newburg and

drank champagne, the family Christmas Eve tradition, and we listened to medieval carols as we unwrapped tinsel and lights to trim the tree.

This is when the moment of truth came. My friend's mother handed me an an ornament and urged me to be sure there were no naked spots on the tree.

I was seized with panic. How could I tell this woman that I'd never done this before? How could I explain to her that when I put the ornament on the tree, a flying ham, all the way from Flatbush, might come crashing through their Oxford window?

"Oy," I muttered to myself, took a deep breath, and placed the ornament at a naked spot in the center of the tree.

The house remained standing. The carols went on playing. No bushes spontaneously combusted and no flying hams pelted the window.

Since that night I've decorated many a friend's tree, sorted many a strand of tinsel, exchanged many a gift. But in my house, my own home, I have no tree, no colored lights, no tinsel. I know they're playing songs of love, but they're still not for me.

However, if I ever get up enough chutzpah, I'd really like to hang a giant twinkling reindeer out my sixth-floor apartment window.

Winner Take All

I dreamed I accepted the Tony Award wearing a CAMP EUGENE O'NEILL sweatshirt. It was an odd dream for two reasons. First, because my friend William Ivey Long, the costume designer, had made me a dress for the occasion; and, second, because until 1989 the only thing I'd ever won was a babka cake at a bakery on Whalley Avenue in New Haven.

My world view has always been from the vantage point of the slighted. I am the underachiever who convinces herself that it's a source of pride *not* to make the honor roll. Still, for the rest of my life I will remember the name of all those people who *did*. I am a walking Where Are They Now column. I'm perpetually curious as to what happened to all those supposed prodigies who were singled out while I and my coterie of far more interesting malcontents passed on.

As a child, on the eve of any school evaluation, I would inform my parents which of my teachers "hated me." In retrospect, it seems doubtful that I was offensive enough to evoke my teachers' animosity, but I certainly wasn't diligent enough in my schoolwork to earn their admiration, either. So, having fashioned a life based on anticipated exclusion—my date left with the blond; they gave the prize to the boy; the woman in the Anne Klein suit and the legs got the job—it came as a genuine surprise, a shock, when, for the first time ever, the winner was me.

On a gray March afternoon, I'm sitting in my bed, looking at my typewriter and thinking about how my life hasn't changed significantly since I was sixteen. I'm working up to a frothy, self-recriminating how-have-I-gone-wrong when the phone rings. On days when I'm building up to substantial negativity, I usually don't pick up the receiver but instead just listen as the messages are recorded. This time, though, the voice belongs to Marc Thibodeau, the press agent for my play *The Heidi Chronicles,* and I like him, so I pick up.

"Wendy, you just won the Pulitzer Prize."

And you, Mr. Thibodeau, are the king of Rumania.

"It's a rumor, Marc. It's just a rumor!" I begin hyperventilating. I am a woman in her thirties wearing a quilted bathrobe, half working, half lying in bed in a room cluttered with assorted stuffed animals. I am not a Pulitzer Prize winner. Edward Albee is a Pulitzer Prize winner.

Mr. Thibodeau informs me that I should call a reporter from the Associated Press. Also, I must call my mother. I begin to dial gingerly. It's possible I am having delusions of grandeur. It's possible I might shortly be calling the *Times* as Eleanor of Aquitaine. Michael Kuchwara, the AP reporter, accepts my call, however, and validates the story. Suddenly I remember sitting in our living room with my mother and watching an episode of the TV series "The Millionaire." I recall how my mother knocked on the television screen to encourage a delivery to our Brooklyn address. "Mother," I want now to shout, "Michael Anthony called *me*. John Beresford Tipton is giving me the Pulitzer Prize!"

Immediately, *everything* changes. The phone rings with the constancy of the American Stock Exchange. Flowers and champagne arrive in competitive quantities. (Since that day I have, in fact, become an expert on the comparative floral arrangements of Surroundings, Twigs, and the Sutton East Gardens.) My doormen are more than taken aback by the flow of deliveries to my apartment. One of them asks me when I'm getting married; another expresses amazement that so many of my friends have remembered my birthday. Eventually, my sister telephones to say that not only has my mother called my aunts to inform them that I've won the Nobel Prize, but my cousins have already begun asking when I'm going to Stockholm.

I will never forget that day. Although I consider myself a professional malcontent, I can't deny at least this one experience of pure, unadulterated happiness. I take a cab to the theater to see the cast of my play, and the whole process of creating the production flashes in front of me. I remember rewriting scenes between bites of cheeseburger as I sat alone at a coffee shop on Forty-second Street. There's something soothing about such inauspicious beginnings. If I concentrate on the coffee shop, I convince myself, I will not be overwhelmed by what is happening to me.

Joan Allen, our leading lady, suggests that I come onstage at the end of the performance. I tell her it's impossible, I'm much too shy. I've never taken a curtain call. I want an *Act One* experience. I want to be watching from the back of the theater.

At intermission, however, I find myself in the lobby face to face with Edward Albee. We know each other from the Dramatists Guild and have friends in common. He embraces me and asks me whether I'll be taking a curtain call. I shake my head. I giggle. Edward then tells me to be a person, to take off my coat and seize the moment.

Walking out onto the stage at the Plymouth Theater I become a character in someone else's script. A part of me imagines that I'm Carol Channing—I want to enter with my arm stretched to the ceiling, shouting, "Dolly will never go away again!" Another part of me has no idea what to do onstage while the audience is applauding. I begin to kiss every actor in my play. As long as I'm moving, I won't have to speak or, heaven forbid, curtsy. That night the audience gives us a standing ovation.

Nineteen eighty-nine was my favorite year so far. Perhaps it is all attributable to the astral plane, Libra in orbit, or Maggie Smith's inability to open as scheduled in *Lettice & Lovage* (which freed the Plymouth Theater for *The Heidi Chronicles*). For whatever reason, I spent the greater part of the spring of 1989 winning awards, as if to counteract on a massive front any remnants of ironic negativity. At the Outer Critics Circle Awards, my escort, the actress Caroline Aaron, whispered to me toward the end of the evening, "Wendy, it's just you and Baryshnikov left." Frankly, I would never have suspected that the two of us might be on a double bill.

Of course, there's also the down side. Will anything this wonderful ever happen to me again? How many people are now going to hate me? Where do I take all these things to be framed? Is it gauche to put them up on the walls in my apartment? What happens if Werner Kulovitz at Barbara Matera's, a theatrical costume shop, has stopped importing that feather-light apparatus to "lift and separate" when I need my next formal? And the nagging "Can *I* ever do it again?"

I haven't actually counted the awards, but I'm sure that if I did I could psych myself into some new form of anxiety over them. In the past I've given my parents every diploma or certificate I've received for them to display in their den. But this time I've been selfish—the awards are still resting in a corner of my study. Some days I ignore them in a concerted effort to get back to my life and work, to return to the point of view of the slighted. But, truthfully, there are times when I wander in and take a surreptitious peek at that corner. Nothing is quite as gratifying as recognition for work one is truly proud of.

As for next year, I will be very hurt if I don't win the Heisman Trophy.

Boy Meets Girl

On a spring morning in 1972, a senior at the Spence School was in Central Park, completing her science project on the reproductive cycle of flowering plants, when she saw an unmarked bus drop off twenty women in silk suits, bow ties, and sneakers on the corner of Eighty-ninth Street and Fifth Avenue. The girl took note; when she was in sixth grade, sneakers and suits had been cause for suspension.

Meanwhile, on the West Side, a middle-aged but very nice lady was on her way to Barney Greengrass, the Sturgeon King, on Eighty-ninth Street, when three cars—a Volvo, a BMW, and a Saab with M.D. plates and a "Save the Whales" bumper sticker—pulled up to Eighty-seventh Street and Amsterdam Avenue. Fifteen young men, whom the lady thought she recognized from her son's protest days at the University of Wisconsin, emerged from the cars. Before the gracious lady could offer them an Entenmann's cake, they jogged into a dilapidated brownstone and immediately began exposing brick and hanging spider plants.

And the city embraced these pioneers, who were dressed in 100-percent-natural fabric. They prospered and they multiplied. From the now infamous drop-offs grew a new breed of New Yorkers, the Professionalites. Only their ratio of men to women, three to four, has remained constant.

What follows is a Love Story in One Act and Six Scenes between two of these sabra Professionalites: Dan and Molly.

Characters

MOLLY. Thirty-three years old, single, successful, and quietly desperate. Every Saturday night, Molly sheds her doctorate in molecular microchips and slips into a Zandra Rhodes macromini. On the weekends, Molly is just another girl at The Trading Post, a popular café on the Columbus Avenue strip. Just another S.S.D.B.G. (Single/Successful/Desperate/Bachelor Girl) waiting for a discriminating Root Canal Man to invite her for an unfulfilling weekend at his summer share in the Hamptons. Molly, a native New Yorker, has recently begun considering relocating to the Sun Belt.

DAN. A successful creative director at B.B.D. & O. advertising agency. He is thirty-two, single, and having a ball. Every night, after twelve hours of Clio Award–winning work for his clients, Dan goes to the Odeon, where he eats poached salmon on grilled kiwi fruit at a table crowded with visual artists, conceptual artists, and performing artists. And every night, after picking up the tab, Dan swears that he, too, will one day give up his job and devote himself to art.

DR. SUSAN. Molly's psychiatrist.

STANLEY TANNENBAUM, PH.D. Dan's psychologist.

HER MAJESTY, THE QUEEN. Ruler of the Helmsley Palace.

Scene One

One night in late August, Dan has a yearning to talk to someone who knows Donna Karan but has moved on to Issey Miyake. Dan slips into The Trading Post, where the number of single women is a plague to the West Side zoning committee. It is here that he first sees Molly, seated at the bar. She is young, she is urban, she is professional. He knows immediately that Molly is the kind of new-fashioned girl he could bring home to his analyst's couch. Dan sits next to her.

DAN Hi.

MOLLY Hi.

DAN Do you come here often?

MOLLY Never.

DAN I don't either.

MOLLY I'm waiting here for a friend. She selected this place. I think what's happening to the West Side is outrageous.

DAN This is really an East Side singles kind of restaurant.

MOLLY   Yes, but it's here on the West Side, so we have to deal with it.

DAN   You sound like a concerned citizen.

MOLLY   Did you ever read any Kenneth Burke? In college, maybe? Lit. Crit.?

DAN   *(Immediately)* Oh, sure.

MOLLY   He divides people into observers, spectators, and participants. I'm here strictly as a sociological observer. I love to watch people in New York. Otherwise I would never come to a place like this.

DAN   I wouldn't either. In my spare time I write film criticism.

MOLLY   *(More interested)* Oh, you're a critic! Who do you write for?

DAN   I write for myself. I keep a film criticism journal.

MOLLY   I love film. Women in film particularly interest me. My favorites are Diane Kurys, Doris Dörrie, and Lee Grant.

DAN   I love women in film too.

MOLLY   *(Impressed)* You're so direct and forthcoming. What do you do?

DAN   I'm a psychiatrist.

MOLLY   Individual, group, house calls?

DAN   Actually, I'm a creative director at the B.B.D. & O. advertisting agency. But I think of it as psychology. Dealing with the individual's everyday dreams and desires. I'm in charge of the Scott Paper account.

MOLLY   Fascinating. I use tissues a lot. I've always wondered why.

DAN   What do *you* do?

MOLLY   I'm a systems analyst for American Express.

DAN   "Do you know me?"

MOLLY   *(Very straightforward)* Not very well. But I'd like to.

DAN   *(Looks at her intently)* Why don't we go some-where a little less trendy to talk. I can tell these aren't your kind of people.

MOLLY   No, I don't belong here. This isn't my New York.

DAN   *(Helps her on with her coat)* That's a nice jacket.

MOLLY   Donna Karan. But I've moved on to Issey Miyake.

DAN   *(Putting on a multilayered karate jacket)* We have so much in common.

MOLLY   "It's a phenomenon." That's a quote from a song in *Gypsy*. "Small world, isn't it?" I love Stephen Sondheim.

DAN   I'm afraid I don't know much about theater. I'm a workaholic. You know, mid-thirties New York guy, longing for Real Relationship with Remarkable Woman, meanwhile finds fulfillment through his work.

MOLLY   I think I like you. But be careful, I have Fear of Intimacy.

DAN   The Bachelor Girl's Disease. I hear it's an epi-demic.

MOLLY   I'm working with my shrink to get past it.

(Pause as Dan looks at her)

DAN   I think I like you, too.

(They begin to exit restaurant)

DAN   What about your girl friend?

MOLLY   Uh, ah, she told me if she wasn't here by now she wasn't coming.

DAN   Not a very reliable friend.

MOLLY   No, but she's working with her shrink to get past it.

(They exit)

Scene Two

Phil's Risotto, a risotto and cheese emporium. Dan and Molly stroll over to the counter arm in arm. It is mid-September.

DAN *(Ordering at the counter)* We'll have lemon risotto, chanterelle risotto, spinach risotto salad, pesto tart, carrot ravioli, goat cheese, goat cheese with ash, and a half pound of American.

MOLLY *(Surprised, almost disturbed)* American?

DAN Have you ever had real American cheese? Not the stuff they sell at the supermarket, but real American. *(He gives her a piece)* Taste this.

MOLLY *(Tasting)* Oh, that's marvelous!

DAN I've been rediscovering American food: peanut butter, grape jelly, Marshmallow Fluff, Scooter Pies, Chef Boyardee, bologna. It is unbelievable! If it's done correctly.

MOLLY *(Softly)* I love you.

DAN Excuse me?

MOLLY I love blue. I adore Kraft blue cheese dressing.

DAN Well, if it's done correctly.

Scene Three

Molly in the office of her psychiatrist, Dr. Susan. It is October.

MOLLY *(Sneezes)* Excuse me. I'm getting a cold.

DR. SUSAN How do you feel about that?

MOLLY Terrible. Tissues remind me of him. He says people should live together before they get married.

DR. SUSAN How do you feel about that?

MOLLY   Sigourney Weaver and Glenn Close are married.

DR. SUSAN   How do you feel about that?

MOLLY   Living together was for kids in the late sixties and seventies. I'm a thirty-three-year-old woman.

DR. SUSAN   How do you feel about that?

MOLLY   I need a commitment. I want a family. I don't want to take a course at the New School on how to place a personal ad. Meryl Streep has three children already.

DR. SUSAN   Why do you always compare yourself to movie stars? You're not an actress.

MOLLY   That's true. That's really true!! That's an incredible insight. Maybe my mother wanted me to be an actress. I hate her.

Scene Four

Dan in the office of his psychologist, Stanley Tannenbaum, Ph.D. It is November.

DAN   I don't think I want to make a commitment to Molly, but I'm afraid of what she'll say.

STANLEY TANNENBAUM, PH.D.   Well, let's put Molly in this chair, and then you can answer for her.

DAN   All right. *(Talking now to an empty chair)* Molly, I don't think I want to make a commitment.

(Dan gets up and sits in chair to answer as Molly would)

DAN   *(Pretending he's Molly)* That's okay. I'm an observer. This is all a sociological investigation. Kenneth Burke divides people into spectators, partici——

(Dan runs back to his seat to answer Molly)

DAN   *(Angry)* Who the hell is Kenneth Burke? That is so pretentious, Molly!

DAN   *(As Molly)* Not as pretentious as keeping a journal of film criticism.

DAN   *(Furious)* You resent my writing! You want to swallow me up. If I live with you, I won't be here anymore. I'll lose myself.

STANLEY TANNENBAUM, PH.D.   Did you hear what you just said?

DAN   I have it. Goddamn it! I have it. Fear of Intimacy. That Bachelor Girl's Disease. Why couldn't I just get burn-out?

Scene Five

Central Park West. The Thanksgiving Day Parade. Dan and Molly are watching floats of Bullwinkle and Super-man pass by.

MOLLY   *(Overcome by the sight of the floats)* I love this parade. Gosh, I really love this parade. Reminds me of growing up here and of New York before there were Benetton shops and a Trump Organization.

DAN   I never imagined people actually grew up in New York.

MOLLY   It was different then. There were real neighborhoods. The ladies on Madison Avenue wore white gloves and ate mashed potatoes at the Kirby Allen Restaurant. Marjorie Morningstar and her family gathered for Sabbath dinners on Central Park West. All artists wore turtlenecks and played bongo drums in the Village. And every night at seven o'clock, men in top hats and tails tap-danced from Shubert Alley to the Winter Garden Theater.

DAN   Really!

MOLLY   Well, I like to think so. Now everywhere I go all the women look like me.

DAN   What's so bad about that?

MOLLY   Nothing, it's just that it's all the same. I like the idea of a flower district, a theater district, a diamond district. The whole city is being renovated into Molly district. Dan, I have to confess. I hate goat cheese.

DAN   *(Softly)* Me, too. But I love you.

MOLLY   Hmmmmmm?

DAN   I hate goat cheese, but I love blue. Molly, with Bullwinkle as my witness, I want to marry you. And every Thanksgiving we can bring our children here. And someday they'll tell someone they met at The Trading Post, "I love this parade, I grew up here."

MOLLY   *(No longer wistful)* But will our children go to Trinity or the Ethical Culture School? They could probably learn Chinese at Trinity, but there are a lot of Wall Street parents. Ethical Culture is nice, but maybe it's too liberal, not enough attention to the classics. How 'bout Brearley? There's something to be said for an all-women's education. *(She kisses Dan)* Dan, just think! We can raise a family of women filmmakers!!!!!

Scene Six

The Helmsley Palace. The Grand Ballroom. An enormous wedding party. Dan and Molly are standing under the altar before Her Majesty, the Queen.

QUEEN   Dan, do you take this woman to be your wife? To love, be emotionally supportive of, have good dialogue with, as well as a country home in the Hamptons, Connecticut, or possibly upper New York State?

DAN I do.

QUEEN Molly, do you take this man to love, and at the same time maintain your career, spend quality time with the children, and keep yourself appealing by joining the New York Health and Racquet Club?

MOLLY I do.

QUEEN *(Addressing the wedding guests)* I've known this couple for two hours. But I've stood guard at their honeymoon suite. Molly will be able to see her makeup in soft light in the bathroom mirror. Dan will be put at ease by the suit hangers that detach from the closet. And if Dan and Molly decide to get remarried someday, and return to the honeymoon suite, I will keep a note of their room number. I wouldn't sleep in a new room, why should they?

DAN *(Bows)* Thank you, Your Majesty.

MOLLY *(Curtsies)* Thank you, Your Majesty.

QUEEN And now by virtue of being Queen of all the Helmsleys, I pronounce you husband and wife. Congratulations! You may kiss the bride. *(Dan kisses Molly. There are cheers and the band begins to play "Lullaby of Broadway." Five hundred men in top hats and tails begin to tap down the aisle)*

Epilogue

Dan and Molly became bi-island (Manhattan and Long), with bi-point three children (a girl, a boy, and an au pair from Barnard), and bi-career (a shift into management for him, a cottage industry for her). As Molly approached middle age she began to consult crystals about her hormonal convergence and undertook frequent pilgrimages to Stonehenge. Dan continued to pursue his interest in early American comestibles, and was featured on the cover of *Just Say Cheese* magazine for his distinguished cellar of American pasteurized-cheese foods.

The fortunes of the Queen, however, followed a crueler path. After a long and glorious reign, she was found to be poaching, thereby violating the charter, and was forced to abdicate. Even a monarch must obey the laws of the realm. On the day she was dethroned, she received a monogrammed Cartier sympathy note from Molly.

Dear Your Majesty,
     Dan and I send you our best wishes at this difficult time.

Molly

PS Is your estate in Greenwich for sale?

Molly's mother had taught her that a lady always sends a note.

Otherwise—apart from twenty years of couples therapy, his-and-her reconstructive surgery, one triple bypass, and four extramarital affairs—they lived happily ever after.

About the Author

Wendy Wasserstein, who has lived most of her life in New York City, was educated at Mount Holyoke College and the Yale School of Drama. Her plays include *Uncommon Women and Others*, *Isn't It Romantic*, and, most recently, *The Heidi Chronicles*, winner of the 1989 Tony Award for Best Play and the 1989 Pulitzer Prize for Drama.